Jaclyn,
Happy Birthday
Enjoy this book...
is Josphat's trainer since
6 years old. We weend you to be
inspired! Love Grandpa Greg
Aunt [?]
& [?] Blair
Bailey
xo
o

Jaclyn,
Have a Great
Birthday!
Melissa

To my parents, Mel and Jan Ames, for their years of sacrifice and support, offered with such overwhelming love.

And to my clients, past and present, who expressed confidence in my program, entrusted me with their horses, and allowed me the opportunity to make them into champions.

CONTENTS

◄◦►

INTRODUCTION

———◄○►———

The idea for this book came about when I was asked how Breed Show Hunter Under Saddle classes differ from the Open USA Equestrian (formerly AHSA) rail classes and the contrasting ways in which these horses are schooled and shown.

My immediate answer was that breed show horses are taught to travel in a self-carriage mode. This comes about by teaching a horse to use his shoulders, back, rib cage, and haunches so that he can attain and maintain his frame by himself. He is round in his back, from his withers to the croup, utilizing his hocks well up under his belly while maintaining a relaxed head and neck carriage. He carries *himself* around the show pen, rather than relying on the rider for total support and balance. The result is a beautiful balance that creates an almost effortless picture of long, low strides and sweeping movement. The horse's head and neck are surfed (stretched) out, his topline is level, his shoulders are up, his back is round, and his hocks are engaged. There is very little reliance on the bridle for support.

In contrast, the Open (USA Equestrian) style concentrates more on keeping a horse quite engaged in the bridle and more elevated. For the most part, this is a precursor to having the horse in the frame necessary to jump, because the emphasis at the open shows is geared more toward hunter and jumper classes.

But, at breed shows, most of the hunter under saddle horses will never see a course of fences. Their careers will keep them on the rail and possibly in pattern work for equitation classes. If breed show horses do go on to classes over fences, what they have learned about using their bodies will benefit them greatly in being able to move beautifully between jumps.

As with any hunter horse, the historic principle of the Breed Show Hunter Under Saddle class resonates in the foxhunt. Hunter under saddle horses became popular as the sport of foxhunting originated in Europe and then came to America in early Colonial times. The idea of hounds chasing the fox (or a coyote, as a substitute, in some parts of North America), and huntsmen on horses following the hounds in pursuit makes for an exhilarating sport. With this in mind you can appreciate the necessity for horses to have long, low, ground-covering strides with the ability to jump brush, fences, ditches, or other obstacles they may encounter. Hence breed show organizations, keeping the heritage of the hunt-seat horse in mind, define their rail hunter under saddle classes as having a horse that moves with a long, low stride reaching forward easily and smoothly. The Breed Show Hunter Under Saddle class is judged on the rail, without the horses going over any fences. This is a preliminary class that could lead to fence work in the future if the competitor desires.

When I work with students on learning the breed show hunter under saddle style, I'm quite frank with them. If they enter an open show with a USA Equestrian judge scoring them, there is a good chance they won't win their open show classes, because the judge will be looking for the USA Equestrian style, possibly perceiving the breed show style as the horse's head carriage being too low and too uncollected in the bridle.

So, as the idea for this book germinated, I thought of the many "breed show people" who can benefit from learning how to be successful at exhibiting in the Hunter Under Saddle classes at Quarter Horse, Paint, Pinto, Appaloosa, Palomino, or Buckskin and Dun shows.

Melissa and her Jack Russell terriers, Jack and Jenna.

We are seeing a movement in the breed show industry of specialization between hunter under saddle and Western horses. Those striving to produce specialized hunter under saddle horses are infusing
more Thoroughbred lines into their stock horses in order to create a
leaner and taller horse. The ultimate goal is to produce a horse with
a nice slope of shoulder, increased leg length, and, ultimately, increased length of stride.

In contrast, there is still a need for the more traditional stock horse
in the all-around world of competition. There are many people who
enjoy riding in several events and have just one horse to fulfill this as-
piration. It may be that they are riding a Western pleasure-type horse
in hunt-seat classes, or a hunter under saddle type in Western horsemanship.

Amateur or youth riders are showing many of these horses. This in-
tensifies the need for breeders to produce horses that are highly train-
able, willing, and good minded, no matter what their type might be.

Some individuals will be starting with two-year-olds, specialized
for one pen or the other. Others will be reschooling older horses on

the basics. And many will be learning to take Western pleasure horses into the hunter under saddle pen to gather those extra points needed for the coveted all-around awards.

This book is for all of you.

God Bless,
Melissa Sexton

{ 1 }

MY TRAINING
PHILOSOPHY

◄○►

This is *your* chance to understand what is behind the progression of training and showing techniques contained in this book. Horses are often misunderstood. My wish is that you understand them well before heading for the round corral or arena. My training program is based on respect and communication, as opposed to threats and abuse. Today's specialized hunter under saddle horses, with their strong infusion of Thoroughbred breeding, will not tolerate abuse. They're brighter and more sensitive than the more cold-blooded show horses that have been out there over the years. Today's horse knows when he's getting a bum deal.

Specialized or not, I don't like to see any horse subjected to intimidation or abuse. We must learn to respect them for the intelligent animals that they are, and mold our training programs to their physical and mental needs. Also, we need to study and understand their innate traits toward herd behavior. I'll provide scenarios to explain how some things that might be considered "training problems" actually stem from instinctive herd behavior.

No Thirty-Day Wonders

Before starting this training program, one must realize that this is a long process. That is the magic word—process. Think of the young

My training program is based on respect and communication.

horse's education in the same way as a child who starts in kindergarten, then learns, grows, and matures into an adult, successfully moving through grade levels and on to graduate school. Each level of schooling is an exciting adventure, as the student graduates from one level of learning to the next. The horse will also go through "grade levels" and stages in his development.

Many of the horses seen at breed shows, even at the World Show level, are in their teens. There are even some still being successfully exhibited well into their early twenties. They may not have been superstars at two, three, or four, but they are superstars in terms of longevity. This is what I love to see. My goal is to get horses truly well trained by using a similar progression from "kindergarten" through "graduate school" that will produce an outstanding product owners and riders can enjoy for years and years.

There's no way that a three-year-old horse with the equivalent of a first- or second-grade education can be as solid and reliable as an older horse with years of show pen experience, which could be compared to a high school or college degree. A young horse isn't physically strong or mentally sound enough to be excessively pressured to perform flawlessly in numerous events. He needs time to progress through all of the training and experiences necessary for him to become well trained.

I'm grateful that my clients over the years have given me the time to bring their horses along slowly. By year three of my training program my clients' horses are solid on the rail, perform nice flying lead changes, and are diversifying into the advanced classes of trail, Western riding, hunt-seat equitation, and horsemanship. By their third year of training they have sailed through graduate school. They truly like their jobs, which is one of the main reasons they've realized a high level of showing success over their careers, winning local, state, and national titles and awards. I've kept my expectations in line with where they are in their education level, and maintained a positive learning environment and attitude to facilitate that learning.

I feel that sometimes riders who are ultracompetitive get in a hurry to win. They put excessive amounts of pressure on a young horse to perform above the horse's current ability level. The risk of this unrealistic expectation is in stressing the youngster until he is unable to handle it, and he mentally explodes under the pressure.

Please don't misunderstand me. I like showing and judging young, talented horses. But it pains me to see talent overexerted. Potential stars of the show pen often give up and their careers end at a young age, when all they needed was time and the patience of an understanding rider.

Consistent self-carriage takes time to acquire. It's going to take a horse at least two years under saddle to learn how to consistently and continually bend, yield, move his shoulders and hips, round his back, drop his head, and maintain his frame without excessive aid from the rider.

My hope for the horse industry is that owners, riders, and trainers don't have unrealistic expectations for two- or three-year-olds that are just getting started in their show careers. These youngsters need patience and forgiveness. Every horse matures at a different rate, both mentally and physically. If your horse isn't ready for the first futurity or show event of the year, please don't get discouraged. Be patient and watch as he comes into himself and becomes more experienced.

As you are showing these young horses, you need a plan to put into place if you get that horse into the show pen and he falls apart. It's like watching a child at her first dance recital when she forgets her routine, stumbles, or just "zones out."

If this sort of thing happens to your young hunter under saddle horse, you'll need to help him rebalance through your hand, seat, and leg aids, which tells him, "Hey—I'm here to help." It's important to be patient and allow your horse time to get himself back into a rhythm. He'll know he can rely on you to help him through— to help him learn eventually to be consistent. As long as you keep thinking in terms of education and progression, you will maintain your horse's trust and he will accept your help.

Remember that a young horse is not only learning the routine, at the same time he's also building the muscle tone and strength needed to perform that routine.

How Herd Behavior Will Affect Training and Showing

Horses are by nature lazy, curious, and gregarious. By gregarious, I mean that they are very much herd oriented. They want to be in a herd, because they are prey animals and there is safety in numbers. I find when working with young horses traits of herd behavior often crop up, and a horse has trouble focusing when being ridden in the arena all by himself. Later in this book, you'll see how it benefits the horse to spend some time riding alone and other times when other horses are in the arena. Especially for those alone times, however, it is important to establish yourself as the "leader of the herd" so that the horse can relate to you and gain confidence from your guidance.

A herd behavior problem that will manifest itself in the show arena occurs when a group of horses—or even one horse—passes the one you're riding. Your horse might try to catch up, or stay paced with the horse that passed him. For example, one of my three-year-olds was at her very first outing in a Green Hunter Under Saddle class at a show in Nevada. She started this behavior on the second track, after the horses had reversed from the first direction of travel. She would canter soft and nice, but then the other horses would pass her and she would try to keep pace with them, getting very bothered if she couldn't. She was probably sending a message to the other horses, "Woo hoo! Wait for me! I'll race ya."

Not only was this a herd behavior trait, but it also came from being green and insecure, and not having the confidence to know that she could stay by herself on the rail. As Kermit the Frog sang, "It's not easy being green."

I don't think a young horse should be aggressively reprimanded for this behavior. In a schooling class, I will quietly pull the horse down to a stop and back it up a few steps, which interrupts his current thought pattern. It gets the message through that, "We're going to canter by ourselves."

If this behavior pops up at a show and surprises you, you can go back to basics at home and teach a horse to work through it. Put the horse in a group setting. Have somebody ride past him. If your horse reacts, stop him, back him up, and get his focus away from the other horses and back onto you. Then when he gets to the schooling show class or the warm-up arena at a breed show, and other horses pass him, hopefully he will be thinking, "Oh, yeah, I remember this from when I was at home. I'm going to stay cadenced and let that horse go ahead of me." If he doesn't remain cadenced in the warm-up pen, stop him quietly, back him up, and then restart. Pretty soon, he'll get the idea from these warm-up schooling exercises that he is to maintain his cadence while being exhibited in the show arena.

Being passed isn't the only problem that rings of herd behavior. Another issue in the show pen deals with nervousness and timid tendencies in horses that consider themselves at the lower end of the herd hierarchy and get caught in show pen traffic.

Let's say there are three horses in the same general area in an arena. One is headed to the rail. You're in the middle with your horse. The third horse should cut off a little at the corner to give you some space, but that doesn't happen and you're trapped for two or three strides. A timid horse will want to back off, possibly stop, and generally overreact to the situation. A more aggressive horse would have no problem going through the tight space. But if your youngster was the mild and meek horse that was tromped on one too many times by a brute in the pasture, he will be very apprehensive about being trapped in a show pen situation and resist going though a hole between other horses. It might even bother him to have another horse's tail swished in his face. The task of building this horse's confidence is enormous, even more difficult to fix than the horse that wants to keep pace with other horses.

Ponying your youngster with an older, sturdy, well-broke horse could be the answer to getting him accustomed to having other horses close to him.

Try Ponying

When dealing with a timid horse, the use of ponying, or leading one horse while riding another, can be beneficial in building confidence. You have to use a good, sturdy horse that won't kick or frighten the horse you're ponying alongside him. The green horse will begin to relax as he grows accustomed to having a tail swished in his face and being bumped by another horse. Ponying is something you can start doing with a yearling if he is a timid youngster and you want to resolve some of these issues before you start riding him as a two-year-old.

When you pony your youngster, it's a good idea to alternate sides, so that equal time is spent working him from *both* sides of the pony horse. This helps desensitize both sides of your youngster.

Dealing with Herd-Bound Tendencies

A big part of my program is centered around teaching patience by tying the horses to a wall at the end of my arena or to a sturdy fence. Horses that exhibit lovesick or barn-sour behavior can be a problem both at home or at a show when they scream and paw each time they're taken away from other horses. They are suffering from a lack of confidence; they think they cannot exist on their own. Imagine trying to ride this horse in the show pen while he screams at his buddies back in the stabling area.

This behavior is definitely associated with herd behavior and the prey/predator programming in these horses. And it can be resolved.

These horses need to learn that they can survive isolation. At home, I will not put such a horse in a stall right next to another horse's stall. This horse will spend a lot of time tied, off by himself, to help him build confidence in his environment.

Being tied to a wall or a sturdy fence helps to teach horses patience. In cooler months I cover them with a blanket.

I'll put him on a consistent routine. Before each ride, I'll tie him up and wait for him to stop screaming and pawing. When he stops, I will go get him and ride him. Then he will be tied again, off by himself where I can see him, but he's not near other horses. If excessive pawing persists, an option is to teach the horse to stand hobbled. If this is the case with your horse, and you have never used hobbles, I strongly suggest you have an experienced horse person help you the first time. Some horses will act adversely by trying to fight the restriction of hobbles.

Often, just plenty of time being tied develops a horse's patience. And when he is tied, my hands are off him. I'm not standing over him. He sees that I am not the predator that is causing him all this grief, but that he is giving it to himself. He teaches himself that it's all right to be alone for a while. He learns to relax, conserve energy, even sleep. Then when he's quiet, I take him back to the barn. He learns that there is a light at the end of the tunnel, and he'll eventually be near his buddies again after his daily work is done.

Being cast out of the herd, from an equine psychological perspective, is a major threat, because horses without a herd in the wild are the first to be eaten. That's why I use this isolation training technique cautiously, so the message isn't misconstrued due to a horse's innate behavior. Teaching horses not to buddy up is not the same as casting them from the herd. What they learn is to possess manners and independence when they are alone. The reward of this is to return to the "herd."

Seek Out Problems

A good training program is one that seeks out problems instead of avoiding them. Seeking out and solving problems is what helps you to educate your horse, so unless we face the problems, we have no grounds for educating.

It's characteristic of some beginning riders to find a problem with a horse and say, "Oh my gosh, this horse is doing something I don't want him to do." The rider panics and sinks into a submissive state, begging the horse, "I hope you don't do that again." This might be the case with a horse that shies at something, such as a garbage can next to the arena. The submissive rider would avoid riding near it in the future. A more effective approach is to meet the problem head on and say, "Okay, let's deal with this."

If your horse exhibits incorrect behavior, like trying to run off, don't pet him and tell him "easy" in a soft voice or ignore what he's doing. To reward bad behavior just encourages the horse to repeat it. Clear discipline is more effective. In this case of trying to run off, you can repetitively pull and release the direct rein (i.e. your left rein if you want him to move to the left), putting him into a circle. It's more difficult for a horse to travel in a circle than it is to move straight. By circling, you gain control as he slows down. Then you can stop and back him up, which readily reaffirms that he is to respond to your hands and legs. Correct him, then relax your rein and leg pressure and allow him to stand and mentally compute the consequences of his actions. Then move on.

The important adage here is, "Don't make the punishment last longer than the crime." Punishment that is carried on too long loses its effectiveness, and the horse will forget what he did wrong in the first place. He might also view you as being unfair.

Be Flexible in Your Schedule

Riding the same horse at the same time every day certainly has its benefits. Horses work extremely well on schedules and routines. The more structure you can offer their lives, the better. Familiarity with routine helps them become comfortable and fosters learning.

Still, you shouldn't stay so structured in your routine that you have no flexibility. Your horses' lives aren't always going to be the same. For example, when participating at a horse show, you will find that the show schedule deviates from your home schedule. When you go to a big event, like a World Show, you might ride your class at close to midnight, so there is great value in teaching the horse to perform on your time requests, even if they conflict with his meal, nap, playtime, or deep sleep.

When I am facing that sort of situation, I'll ride my horses at weird hours during the four to six weeks before the upcoming show. You'd be amazed at the look you will get from old Snuffy when you take him out of his stall at 4:00 A.M. and throw a saddle on him. He'll stare at you like you died and forgot to lie down, but he needs to have that flexibility in routine to handle the differences that will occur when he hits the show road.

And When *Will* You Hit the Show Road?

I don't get my horses so well-broke at home that I expect them to win the first time out. I expect them to be young and green and do stupid little things in the show pen, like stopping during the canter gait either for no reason or while evacuating his bowel. I need to maintain my perspective here and encourage the horse to relax and refocus while educating him on the proper protocol of the show arena. That's all part of the training it takes to get them seasoned.

Other people might say, "I'm not taking my horse until he's ready."

The problem with this line of thinking is that horses are never completely ready for that first show. You cannot possibly create at home all the horse show stimuli that your horse will be expected to ignore while he focuses on pace, cadence, rhythm, and self-carriage. It's like a child who is taking piano lessons. You don't wait until he's ready for Carnegie Hall before you let him play in a recital. You must give the horse opportunities to get rid of the performance jitters before any expectation of winning can be realized.

With your young horse, just set a date and say, "I'm going to this show and we're going to ride in this class." Then you must follow through. Otherwise, it's too easy to put it off, and that never benefits the horse. Until he figures out why you're working him so much on transitions, self-carriage, and all the other moves, until he can actually be involved in a couple of classes, he has no idea why he's being asked to do all that work.

Take him to a show. Don't worry if he makes mistakes. Evaluate the strengths and weaknesses of his performance, so you'll know what to fix for the next time. So what if he doesn't place too well? Remember, it's his first time out, and training is a long process. Don't expect him to be perfect. Just strive for mastery of the fundamentals to give him the key to success. He's young and green. He still has a long way to go. Take everything in stride and look at the bigger picture.

Putting "first place" pressure on young horses is just too much. They can't live up to that for you. They can't be flawless. If your horse does something understandable like stumbling, be extra patient and understanding. If you hit the panic button, the horse might become scared. In general, horses have a lot of try and really want to please their riders. The real people-pleasers want to give you perfection, but sometimes they're just not able to do it. These young horses are very sensitive individuals that will quit a high-pressure training program because they can't handle negative vibes from their owners and/or riders.

Horses really pick up on the attitudes of their riders. They will love the show pen if their riders love it. However, the opposite also holds true.

Be honest with yourself. You might think your horse is operating at 100% at home, but your expectations might be low there because you're not continually challenging him. It is hard for the horse not to be good at home, in surroundings he is comfortable with. When he is ridden away from home, he's going to be too distracted to work the same way he did in his own arena. So higher expectations may be called for at home, in order to challenge the horse to higher mastery of skills that will increase his accomplishments at the show.

Both in the home arena and when you're seasoning in the show pen, knowing when to challenge your horse versus when to back off can be the determining factor in how successful your training program will be. This fine line between when to pressure for more, and when to back off, will be the toughest obstacle you'll have to deal with during this process. And you will have to deal with it daily.

Learn by riding regularly and taking clues from your horse. Is he resisting by pinning his ears and kicking out when leg pressure is applied? Or is he accepting the leg pressure and moving right off, as he should? Look for reactions to cues to determine if he's ready for the next step, or whether you should regress to easier tasks for a while.

Whether pushing through resistance or backing off, one needs to end each ride on a positive note. If asking for a difficult maneuver, such as your horse's first attempts at a turn on the haunches (explained later in this book), and he takes just one or two correct steps with his front feet, stop, release your hand and leg pressure as a reward, and pet him.

If your horse gets flustered, go back to something he knows well. If schooling at home becomes frustrating, tie him up for a while and let him think through that frustration. Don't panic at his, or your, frustration. By remaining calm and patient, you'll find the correct solution both in and out of the show pen.

When starting to show your green horse and problems arise in the class, don't stress out. My motto is, don't react. Keep the fun in the show pen, let the horse realize how rewarding it can be, and he will excel.

So There You Have It

Now you know what fuels my philosophy on training. As you begin reading my sequence of methods, you'll see how I establish myself as herd boss with personal space exercises and continue the training progression. From the first time I set hands on a horse, we work together towards the greater goal.

I don't try to make a World Champion out of a horse incapable of that feat. But I do want to see him accomplish as much as he has the potential for. And most of all, I want him to love his job. As you embark on this training program with your own horse, work to master the fundamentals and build on that foundation.

{ 2 }

SIZING UP
PROSPECTS

————◄◦►————

If you don't already have a hunter under saddle horse that you're actively showing, maybe you are shopping for a prospect and are looking at youngsters. Or you have a horse in your barn that you have successfully shown in Western classes and would like also to show English. You're wondering if he'll fit the bill. Even before I give you the guidelines for sizing up a prospect, I want you to spend some time considering one important factor. How much horse do you need?

It's simple—choose a horse based on the level of competition at which you will be exhibiting.

Showing at major Regional or World shows requires a lot more horse. The tall, finished, specialized horse with a very Thoroughbred-type appearance and the classic movement required to compete at that level is going to cost big bucks. A younger horse, without months or years of training, will be more affordable.

If you're showing at weekend shows and smaller circuits, you won't need as much horse to be successful as you would for the major shows. It would be nice to have a specialized horse, but your Western horse stands a good chance of getting points at these shows, even though he's not 16.2 hands tall with a swan neck. To show at a local level allows the opportunity to participate in many different categories of classes and not be as restricted in your choices as you would be with a more specialized mount.

Before You Go Shopping

When my clients shop for a hunter under saddle prospect, I suggest they make a list of both their show pen goals and an equine wish list before we begin looking at horses. I tell them to remember that horses are animals and the only truly perfect ones are made of plastic and are on the shelves at Wal-Mart. So, when looking for a real horse, it's important to decide what can or cannot be lived with in terms of disposition, talent, smoothness, vices, trainability, and color. This will help them find a horse with which a partnership can be built.

Can He Convert?

The basic attributes that put a Western horse in the running to compete in hunter under saddle classes come from what has made him successful in the Western pen. He is a good mover, travels flat-kneed, and maintains a level topline.

Let's say you have an older stock-type horse that has shown in Western events. He will be one of two things—short-strided or long-strided.

Both can be equally good Western pleasure horses, because if they've been successful, they are probably slow-legged. The long-strided, slow-legged Western pleasure horse will be easily adaptable to hunt seat and will make a good all-around type of horse that can compete in the hunter under saddle classes, especially if he is consistent in his movement and well-broke. Even though he doesn't have the look of a Thoroughbred, he will still earn some points, particularly at weekend shows. Some breed show judges aren't happy with the specialization from Thoroughbred infusion. They prefer stockier horses, and want their winners to be well-broke and to have given the solid performance of an all-around horse.

A Western pleasure horse that is extremely short-strided but is still slow-legged and flat-kneed might be better suited to cross over to hunt-seat equitation classes at smaller weekend shows. However, I have seen very cute, short-strided horses walk out with the points in the hunter under saddle pen as well. It truly depends on the judge's preference. He might like the fact that this horse has a cute appearance and is very well-broke.

Therefore, there is an avenue for both types of Western-oriented horses. The important thing is to pick shows and judges carefully, especially if chasing points for all-around titles and when showing on a budget. It's beneficial to keep a list of judges who obviously like or dislike your horse based on how they have placed him at shows. In the future, look over your list, and make choices about which shows to attend based on who is judging.

Don't be intimidated if the class is full of big, tall hunt seaters. You can certainly place. Let's say there are some young 16.2-hand or taller horses in a Junior Hunter Under Saddle class. They're not yet so broke or seasoned that they have the consistency and cadence of your seasoned Junior Western-type horse. Maybe it's only the third or fourth time the young hunt seaters have been shown. There are judges who will place a Western horse over that "true hunt seater" because that horse is more seasoned and more functionally correct around the show arena on that given day.

Keep your expectations in line and look at the bigger goal of winning an "all-around" or just having a lot of fun. If you are rewarded with points, wonderful—take them with gratitude!

Looking for a Specialized Prospect

If shopping for your first hunter under saddle prospect, it might warrant taking along an equine professional who is familiar with the breed show industry and hunter under saddle competition. A

This foal is too young to assess as a hunter under saddle prospect, but by the time she is six months old, her conformation will be easier to judge.

professional with a good eye can certainly help make an informed purchase decision.

If looking for the specialized horse with that tall, leggy, Thoroughbred look, you can start sizing up prospects when they're fairly young. Look for correctness of leg, body, head, neck, throat latch, and topline as early as six months of age.

To get a more accurate assessment, I prefer to look at the "babies" when they're long yearlings, and past the irresistible cute baby stage. If one is going to have a short neck or thick throat latch at maturity, it will definitely be apparent. If the neck is long and nice, you'll certainly key in on that feature. And the best part is if you just watch them move out in a pasture or other large area, you can see what heredity has given them in terms of the way they move. When getting that first impression, I'd just as soon not watch a prospect being longed. If he's loose and free I can get a better evaluation of both natural talent and what will need to be enhanced by training. Closer evaluation can then be done on a longe line.

Conformation

I look at a horse's conformation to determine if a prospect will be of a hunter under saddle type, and also as an indication of how well he will be able to perform. A well-conformed horse is more likely to be a good-moving horse. A good prospect should have a nice long neck, a clean throat latch, and a sloping shoulder.

The top of the neck should be twice as long as the underside of the neck. The top of the back should be half as long as the bottom line of his body, from elbow to stifle. This is what sets up a good slope of shoulder. These ratios help to evaluate slope of shoulder: The more slope, the better the stride.

The horse's pastern angle, which is the part between the ankle joint and the coronet band, should be at the same angle as the shoulder.

I like a long neck with a clean throat latch that ties in at the body so that the horse can easily achieve a flat topline. This makes future headset training and overall balance more natural for the horse.

Other factors include:

EYE: I like a large, soft, kind eye. Not only is it attractive, but it is also considered a sign of trainability. A horse with a big "kind eye" is usually less fractious by nature than a "pig-eyed" horse, because the bigger eye has a larger field of vision.

HEAD: We'd all like to have a hunt seater with a pretty face and beautiful head, but don't go out and buy only a face, because movement is still the name of the game. A great-moving, plain-headed, 17-hand horse will still fare extremely well in the hunter under saddle pen.

Oftentimes, a big-headed yearling will grow into his head and ears as he matures. But if he doesn't, it is important to remember that a braided mane and a nice English bridle will work wonders in dressing up a common head. That's why I suggest people don't pass up an otherwise top prospect just because his head isn't classic. Applying equine makeup can make all the difference as well. (See the chapter on "Finishing Touches.")

LEGS: The prospect's legs should be straight and correct, free of blemishes. His hocks should be low and set under the hindquarter, not trailing out behind. I avoid horses with high hocks because they tend to move like a Ferris wheel behind, with a high-stepping motion. The hocks should only be slightly higher than the horse's knees. Visualize an imaginary line from the center of the back of the horse's knee, to the center of the front of his hocks. If his hocks are quite a bit higher, he is out of balance and will likely have a tendency to "travel downhill" and be heavy on his forehand.

KNEES: I avoid the calf-kneed horse. Although he might move flat-kneed as a young horse, there is always the likelihood that he will break down and become lame with continued use and age. In contrast, I avoid the horse that is over at the knees since he typically will not move with a flat knee. He is, however, more likely to stay sound longer. Look for knees that are large and flat, without deviating forward or backward when viewed from the side.

BALANCE: A horse's overall balance will determine if he has the physical coordination necessary to be a successful athlete. To determine balance, step back to get a complete picture of the horse. Assess whether all the parts seem to blend into and belong to one another. A well-balanced horse has a good slope of shoulder, with matching pastern and hip angles.

Evaluating the Walk, Trot, and Canter

The first thing I look for is track up at the walk and trot. "Track up" means that the hind feet step at least into, if not in front of, the front hoofprints. I know that if a horse naturally has this track up, I will be able to build a good hunt seat stride at the trot. He'll also have enough depth of hock for a good canter. If the horse has this natural ability, it's not going to be a battle to get the type of movement I ultimately want him to achieve with a rider on board.

I also look for natural flat-kneed movement both in the trot and canter. By "flat-kneed," I mean that the horse completely extends his front leg before setting it down. He doesn't have a rolling knee motion, but rather lifts through his shoulder and moves with a long, low, fully extended front leg.

One movement trait which might send some buyers running to their cars, while stuffing their checkbooks in their back pockets, doesn't bother me one bit. In fact, I like it. That movement is a big, floating, animated trot, as a horse will have when he's feeling high, and travels with extreme suspension. As long as the horse is flat-kneed, this type of trot shows me how much spring he has in his joints and how much he wants to use that spring to propel himself forward. I don't want him bouncing around the show pen, but suspension will come in handy when I work on adding more length to his already long stride.

At the canter, I want to see this prospect keep his shoulders up and drive with his hocks. At this point, I don't care where he carries his head. If he wants to move with his head up, no problem, because that can be taken care of later on with training.

Sizing Up Size

Today's hunter under saddle horses, especially those with a lot of Thoroughbred in their pedigrees, are definitely taller than most Western horses. If you want to get an idea of how tall a prospect might be when it matures, try the string test. This is not an exact science, but it is close. Most horses are relatively well-proportioned in their bone structure, so you should get at least a ballpark idea of height by "stringing" a young horse.

Hold a string with a plumb weight from in front of the center of the knee down to the coronary band. Next, measure the distance. If it measures 16 inches, that translates to 16 hands. If you

This yearling Paint filly is more a Western than a hunter under saddle candidate: she has a stocky build and is not long legged. She will stand about 15.2 at maturity.

This three-year-old American Quarter Horse filly is very "English" in her appearance, with a lovely head and eye, small throat latch, and a long neck. Long legged, she is likely to finish growing at 17 hands. (Her full brother, a bay two-year-old, appears in the photos in the Round Corral chapter.)

come up with16½ inches, the horse's ultimate height should be
16.2.

String works best because most babies will run for the hills if you
reel out a noisy metal measuring tape and reach for their legs. If
you're out of string, try a nice soft fabric measuring tape. The string
test works from the time horses are babies until they're about two
years old.

Some Useful Terms

"Horse for sale" ads often have terms that describe the attributes of potential show horses. Knowing their meaning will
help you choose a suitable prospect. Watch a young animal
out in the pasture, or traveling free in an arena to see if some
of these positive traits are present in his natural way of going.

• **Slow-Legged:** A horse that carries himself in the correct
  frame utilizes his body and his stride to the fullest. Because he
  uses the full length of his stride, rather than cutting it short
  with unnecessary small choppy steps, his stride is longer. The
  small, choppy stepper is like a tap dancer or a soldier marching on double time. The slow-legged horse is like an ice
  skater performing to slow music. The skater uses long, graceful "steps" to cover the ice. His legs almost appear to be in
  slow motion. His movement is soft and fluid. The same is
  true of a slow-legged horse.

• **Flat-Kneed:** This term is often misunderstood. Some people think it means that the horse travels stiffly and doesn't
  bend his knees at all. Not so. A flat-kneed horse is fluid and
  loose in his movement. He does not "march," or jerk his
  knees high at any gait, or raise his knee any more than necessary to reach his leg forward. Each front leg extends
  straight forward before landing on the ground.

  Because he uses his entire body, the horse doesn't travel
  heavily on his front end like a wheelbarrow. He's more like

a speedboat without the speed. The power comes from behind, so the front end is lifted. The horse is able to lift his
shoulders because the power from behind creates the strong
engagement of his haunches.

Throughout this book you will read about the importance of
a horse "using his shoulders." The best way to learn this concept is to get down on the floor on your hands and knees.
First, move your knees out behind you. That shoves a large
percentage of body weight onto your hands and arms, which
in this case are acting as "front legs." Still on hands and knees,
try "walking" across the floor with knees trailing behind. Your
back will dip, and you'll move in a choppy and stiff manner.
You'll have to lift your "front legs" in an exaggerated manner
to keep from falling on your chin.

Now, position your knees more forward, up under your
belly and toward your navel. Rock back onto your "haunches."
Your back will now "round," like a cat lifting his spine asking
to be petted and scratched. Feel what this change does to your
"front legs." You can now lift your shoulders and easily extend
each "front leg" fully, in a fluid and soft motion with the grace
of Tai Chi or ballet. You don't have to lift your arms high to
take those steps. You just keep them low and reach forward.

Congratulations. You are flat-kneed.

That kind of grace is what we want to see on our hunter
under saddle horses. A stiff-moving horse that jerks his knees
up often has one or more conformation faults. He might be
over at the knees, which simply means his knees buckle forward in front, or he may have a very upright and straight
angle to his shoulders and pasterns. Whatever the reason, a
horse that travels with "too much knee" is not an ideal candidate for the hunter under saddle class.

• **Topline:** A horse that engages from his hindquarters,
rounds his back, and lifts his shoulders is most likely to have

a relaxed head and neck carriage. He is not struggling to move. His topline starts at the poll or the tips of his ears, continues down the length of his neck to the withers, and on to the point of his hip, or croup area. This is a "level topline."

If a horse is not "driving from behind," by engaging his haunches and pushing from behind to move, he might travel very high-headed. His back will arch (downward), rather than round (upward). His hocks don't come up underneath him, but trail out behind. He can't seem to bring those hocks underneath him just as you couldn't with your "back legs" during the floor exercise. He has no impulsion from behind. His head is up much higher than his back and his croup. His topline is not level, and he is not moving in a pretty manner.

Quite the opposite is a horse that moves with his head too low, often no higher than his knees. A few years ago, these horses were called "peanut rollers," which describes the look perfectly. The low head doesn't just destroy the level topline, but also causes the horse to travel heavy in front, again like a wheelbarrow. Rather than pushing and propelling from his haunches, he is pulling himself forward with his front legs.

3

MANAGING THE HUNTER UNDER SADDLE HORSE

———◄❍►———

To properly manage your hunter under saddle horse, you must make informed decisions about his feed, housing, medical, and physiological needs. You'll need a "pit crew" consisting of a veterinarian, farrier, and chiropractor to work together to solve problems and keep your horse healthy and capable of performing. Training problems that might pop up don't just generate from a horse's mind. Oftentimes, it's a pain issue.

Feed, however, is one of those components with a profound effect on both the body and the mind.

At the Dinner Table

Rule number one, especially with a Thoroughbred-type horse, is "Don't feed him like a racehorse, or he'll act like a racehorse." Your hunter under saddle horse will need sufficient body weight, but not a level of excessive energy that keeps him higher than a kite and unable to focus.

While I suggest you consult your veterinarian to formulate your own feeding program, let me tell you what has worked for me over the years, and why.

I feed my horses a high-fat, low-sugar, and low-carbohydrate diet. It is sufficient in amounts and in the nutrients it offers, but low in excessive energy derived from sugars. Energy can be derived from sugars or fats. Energy from sugar is produced in a quick surge from either carbohydrate that changes to glucose (sugar), or from sugars themselves. They metabolize quickly and elevate the blood sugar level, which can leave a horse feeling hyper and less relaxed, especially if he's not being worked hard enough to expend the energy load.

The effects of energy from fat provide a more soothing effect on the horse because of the slower, more even metabolic rate. It's a "time-release" effect rather than a "candy bar hit."

The energy required by a mature hunter under saddle horse is at a "maintenance to light-working" level. He doesn't need the energy load required of a rapidly growing youngster, or a cutting or reining horse.

A horse with a lot of Thoroughbred in him that is loaded with a high-sugar diet ends up with a lot of behavior problems that could be solved if his feed produced less sugar energy. A horse with far too much energy is easily distracted and difficult to deal with. It will seem to take eons on the longe line to work out the excess energy before he is ready to ride. That's not good for his mind, body, or legs.

On the other hand, a high-fat diet keeps the energy load off of a horse, so he can have a good mind, but also maintain the proper weight to look good in the show pen.

These horses need a good body score. (See sidebar.) On a scale of one to nine, I prefer my hunter under saddle horses to have a score of about five or six. If you're starting to see every rib, his hipbones sticking out, and the horse's tailhead protruding from his croup, this horse is not healthy enough to carry you around the pen.

The opposite of the horse with too much energy is the one that is starved down so he'll feel lethargic. A few years ago at breed shows we saw this trend where horses had gone down beyond a "greyhound look." Judges began to penalize those horses for being too thin, recognizing this unfortunate "training" technique of starving them, so they didn't have the energy to do anything bad. This should never re-place getting a horse properly broke.

You have to strike a balance. Keeping horses at the right body score should be a priority. It's not always easy with tall, Thorough-bred-type horses that take more feed than their smaller, stockier, easy-keeper counterparts.

A lot of people get into trouble with premixed feeds that are bound with molasses, a sugar. They get the horse's body weight up, but the mind goes. Here's how I strive to meet that fine line.

Rice bran is one of my feed staples. It is high in fat, it doesn't raise blood sugars, and it is packed with essential oils and natural an-tioxidants that put beautiful, shiny coats on all the horses in my barn. I feed one to two cups of rice bran daily, and even more to horses that are hard to keep weight on. Your veterinarian can make suggestions on how much rice bran to feed a horse that doesn't hold his weight.

Beet pulp is another feed I use instead of premixed grains. It doesn't produce a high energy load, and it is a concentrated calorie source. That makes it an excellent choice for horses that need to gain weight. It's not the easiest feed to use because you have to soak it in water. *Caution! It is not safe to feed beet pulp in its dry form.* Beet pulp starts as a dry pellet that expands tremendously when liq-uid is added, even if that liquid is your horse's saliva or stomach fluid. Choking and colic, due to stomach expansion, are major threats if dry beet pulp pellets are ingested.

The safe way to use beet pulp is to feed it after it has soaked in warm water for at least four hours. The soaking time allows the pellet to soften and become mushy with almost the consistency of a mash.

I prepare beet pulp by putting the dry pellets in a bucket and pouring in warm water to a level that comes two inches above the top of the pellets. If you are at a show and must use cold water, I strongly recommend soaking the pellets overnight, because cold water doesn't expand the pellets as quickly as warm water. Fed properly, beet pulp is an excellent "non-sweet" feed.

Another reason I stay away from "sweet feeds" is that many horses, especially Thoroughbreds, have a susceptibility to being allergic to molasses. It puts them in an almost diabetic state, similar to the prediabetic condition in humans. These horses need feed that won't skyrocket their blood sugar.

I top my concentrate supplement with a well-balanced vitamin/mineral supplement that is high in calcium and the essential amino acid, lysine. This supplement helps make up for the inverse calcium/phosphorus ratio that might occur when feeding grass hay with beet pulp and/or rice bran. Especially with young horses, it is important that you keep that calcium/phosphorus ratio at 2:1 for proper growth of bone, cartilage, and ligaments.

Hay There

During my show season, which lasts about nine to ten months, I rely on high-quality grass hay. It provides adequate nutrition for "rail" horses that don't expend the amount of energy reiners or cutters do. It also helps to keep weight levels up, along with the beet pulp and rice bran. However, it doesn't keep their energy level higher than a kite.

During off-season winter months, I give alfalfa/grass mixed hay to the horses that are not yet mature and still growing—such as the two- and three-year-olds. It gives them a temporary boost of crude protein. Crude protein requirements vary depending on the age of the horse. A weanling needs 13 percent, yearlings need 11 percent, coming two-year-olds require 10 percent, but when it comes to mature horses working lightly, the requirement drops to around 8 percent. I can't see leaving a mature horse on alfalfa year round. Alfalfa is often at least twice as high in crude protein as the recommended levels, so the excess is excreted through their kidneys, which can lead to health problems. Mature horses that have a lot of Thoroughbred breeding are more sensitive, so they are left on grass hay year round, especially those I feel are having difficulty excreting the waste of alfalfa, shown by muscle stiffness and soreness.

When it gets close to show time, usually February, I switch the "alfalfa horses" back to a high-quality orchard or timothy grass hay, to reduce their energy and get them focused on their jobs.

Using Supplements

Where I live, in the Pacific Northwest, hays and pastures are deficient in selenium. I supplement this mineral because selenium-deficient horses will exhibit signs of tying up. Tying up is a condition characterized by lameness and stiffness of muscle groups, primarily through the back, loin, and hip areas. These muscle spasms can become so severe that the horse loses all muscle function, and the muscles themselves become hard as a rock. This is extremely painful for the horse and causes the muscles to break down. Damaged muscle cells release myoglobin, which is in turn excreted from the horse's body through urine. This excretion is recognizable from the dark brown, almost red, color of the urine from an affected horse, rather than the cloudy, pale yellow urine of a healthy horse.

Whenever you supplement your horse with selenium, you must also supplement with its counterpart vitamin E, because both are necessary for proper muscle metabolism. Your area, however, might produce hay and pasture that is high in selenium. Colorado, for example, is one state with a high concentration of selenium in its soil.

Some problems caused by selenium toxicity are: (1) loss of mane and tail hair; (2) a dull coat; (3) brittle hooves which crack, and if not attended to by a veterinarian and farrier, will slough away from the coronary band, causing extreme pain and lameness as the inside of the hoof becomes exposed to the outside environment; and (4) hoof abscesses.

Given these consequences of mineral deficiencies/toxicities, it is extremely important to check with your veterinarian for area-specific recommendations on any supplements that might be necessary.

Your veterinarian can also help you avoid duplicating vitamins and minerals if you use more than one supplement. For example, a premixed grain feed that is fortified with vitamins, to which a vitamin/mineral supplement and a vitamin-based product to produce shiny coats were added, could result in quite an overkill of additives. There are toxicity concerns in overfeeding fat-soluble vitamins such as A, D, E, and K.

Tune In to Possible Soreness and Discomfort

No owner wants to see a horse in pain, but some horses aren't demonstrative when they're hurting. So, as an owner and rider, you have to tune in to your horse's subtleties and look for training and behavior difficulties that might be caused by soreness.

If you're having trouble getting your horse to respond to any part of the training in this book, the first thing to do is ask yourself, "Is my horse hurting?" Not nearly enough people give this problem the attention it deserves.

Horses by nature are not disobedient. They are very much followers and don't want to be bad and incur the herd leader's wrath. Therefore, if your horse is giving you trouble, you need to look at your management program for an explanation for behavior that is not related to training.

When working with young horses, you also have to consider growth spurts. When a horse is growing quickly or not growing level, it's possible for him to become body and joint sore. Many young horses go through these unlevel growth stages where the croup is much higher than the withers. They are "butt high." Later another growth spurt causes the withers to "catch up," and the process is repeated over and over until the horse reaches maturity. If such a horse is two or three inches higher in the croup due to growth, it's easy to see why this temporary out-of-balance condition can cause soreness.

Don't be intent upon riding a young horse seven days a week, every week of the year "no matter what." A rider will often fight with a horse that is sore and stiff and is battling pain, not understanding that the basis of this fight truly is pain. When I have a horse with problems related to a big growth spurt, I give him time off, anywhere from a week to a month, if necessary, in extreme cases. Many of these horses not only retain what they've learned, but come back even better after a break. Think of your own experience as a child at the end of summer vacation—weren't you excited about returning to school?

If your horse is not going through a growth spurt, but you suspect something is wrong, watch him move. If he appears stiff in the stifles or hocks, feel for heat in those joints. You can push on his back or other trigger points, like the loins, and see how he reacts. Just pushing on those areas will cause him to sink down, away from the pressure. When you saddle up, the horse might immediately arch his back in defense. Or he might sink his back in response to pain from a saddle that is pinching him.

When you pull off the saddle and immediately touch the horse's back, he might show you that he's obviously sore, but the next morning he's not. That is usually a sign of a tack problem, but if he's sore that night and the next morning, he might have a problem in his stifles or hocks. All these body parts are intertwined, causing soreness issues that you need to research. Don't hesitate to call your veterinarian for an opinion.

It's normal for a horse in training to experience some soreness because he's building muscle. That's why, after day three or four of initial training, I rest him for a couple of days so I'm not fighting him through the expected muscle soreness typical in any athlete. The idea is simple: A sore horse needs time off, and the owner needs to investigate the cause of pain. We, as trainers, are developing athletes who need recovery time to continue positive growth.

If soreness seems to be more pronounced than you'd expect, it might be time to call the chiropractor.

Could It Be a Chiropractic Problem?

Problems that might at first be construed as training resistance can actually be chiropractic in nature. Looking at your horse as the athlete he is, if he's going to reach his maximum potential, chiropractic care has to be just as high on the list of regular care as dental work, shoeing, worming, vaccinations, and other routine veterinary care.

Among other problems, your horse is not taking a lead. He won't set his head properly, when he has done it before with no problems; now, he wants to carry his head much too high or low. He might drop a shoulder or crossfire behind. A horse that usually gives you a nice long stride no longer seems capable of doing so. He could have an elbow or shoulder out of adjustment. Or he's not working with the depth of hock in the canter as he has done consistently, which can indicate a dropped lumbar vertebra or a floating rib out of adjustment. A horse that becomes cinchy might also have a rib out of adjustment.

The list of places where a horse can be out of adjustment is endless. There are approximately 150 trigger points that reside in the ear alone. If you are having trouble slipping the bridle on, or the horse won't let you clip or even get near his ears with your hand, he is probably screaming for chiropractic relief. Ears that are cold and sore are an indication of blocked circulation within the body.

People miss these signs. Instead, they get mad at the horse and twitch or drug him, especially when clipping. They need to ask why the horse's ears are so sensitive. Why can't you touch his ears, and what can be done to help the horse? Acceptance of clipping is a behavioral skill that has to be taught. It can be taught more easily if the horse can learn it without pain.

Believe it or not, horses can have headaches. A horse that pulls back when he's tied is likely to have major problems at the cervical vertebrae area. Anytime I see a horse that sets back (pulls back and fights his lead rope when tied), I cringe and speed-dial the chiropractor, because I know this horse has just impaired his chances of performing well at the next show. He'll have a headache and will be out of adjustment in the atlas, the first cervical vertebra of the neck. The atlas is connected to balance because of its location in relation to the inner ear. When atlases are out, we see lead problems at the canter and soreness in the loins.

Horse owners who are skeptical about the benefits of chiropractic might say, "The Mustangs of yesteryear didn't have chiropractors, and they survived." Those Mustangs were not confined in stalls or pens. Nor were they halter broke and taught to lead. They were not ridden. They weren't asked to collect and move in the way modern horses must to win in the show pen. And they weren't the sensitive individuals that we see in the hunter under saddle pen today that have a high percentage of Thoroughbred breeding. Simply put, the mustangs were not the athletes today's show horses are.

There's also a definite difference in the way horses react to pain. Mustangs developed the ability to ignore it so they could keep moving across their natural environment to avoid becoming lion bait.

Even today, there are quiet horses that stoically try to ignore pain even though they aren't able to move correctly. However, other horses can "stub a toenail" and think their world is coming to an end.

Your job is to communicate with your horse and try to ascertain the difference between bad behavior and behavior that is pain induced.

And, if that isn't enough, stop and consider dental problems, which often go hand in hand with chiropractic difficulties.

Take Care of Those Pearly Whites

A horse's mouth is constantly changing during his entire lifetime. The horse's teeth are constantly erupting, meaning that they continually grow until the tooth itself is completely worn. That occurs when the horse gets close to thirty-something. Destructive vices such as cribbing or eating sand can speed up the process. However, the majority of changes in a horse's mouth occur between the ages of two and five years, which is when most training occurs. During this time frame twenty-eight permanent teeth in a mare and thirty-two in a stallion or gelding will erupt. The difference in numbers is due to the fact that a male horse will generally have canine teeth where females will not. These numbers also do not take into account the troublesome wolf teeth that can erupt within the horse's first year of life.

A horse eats by biting forage with his incisors (front teeth) and then grinding from side to side with his premolars and molars to crunch and break down the food before swallowing. The grinding causes enamel points to form on the teeth. These points can cut the inside of the horse's cheek and his tongue.

One indication of a dental problem is a horse that opens his mouth when he sets his head. Or he might raise his head before setting it in order to unlock his jaw so it will slide. A problem might be causing the jaw to lock, such as when a long top tooth slides between two molars on the bottom. When a horse sets his head, his bottom jaw naturally slips forward, so if there are any problems in the track of the teeth moving together, the horse will have to move his head in odd ways in order to unlock the jaw and slide it down. In a training program where you're trying to get a correct, consistent head position, this can be quite a problem.

A horse with dental problems might also move with his head cocked off to the side. He might pull through the bit or gap at the mouth. Tossing his head is another way he will react to the discomfort.

The frequency of regular dental care varies. I might have young horses between the ages of one and five, when most changes in the mouth occur, worked on every six months to head off problems before they start. Some horses as young as five to six months get wolf teeth, which are about the size of a pinky fingernail. They are directly in front of the second premolars. Many people confuse wolf teeth with canines. Most male horses have canines and most females do

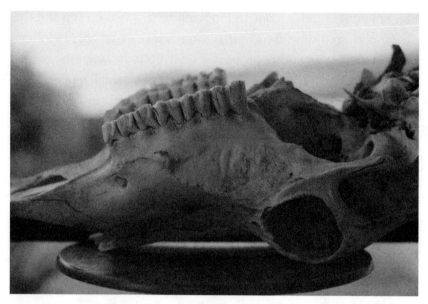

The row of teeth in the foreground is starting to form hooks, but they are not as pronounced as on the teeth in the next photograph.

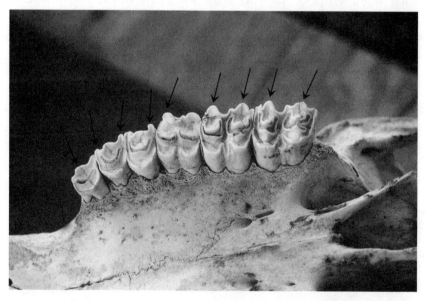

These points can cut the inside of the horse's cheek and his tongue.

not, but either can have one to four wolf teeth—two on top and two on the bottom. I want those out as soon as we can get ahold of them. If wolf teeth, or any other problems, show up in between the regular dental care, I don't hesitate to call for an extra dental appointment.

Even without the typical dental problems of youth, I don't suggest a horse going longer than one year between exams. Spotting problems can sometimes be as simple as a visual check underneath the jaw. Big bumps, especially with young horses, could be from retained caps on the premolars and molars. But the best way to determine if your horse needs dental work is to haul him to the equine dentist or have the dentist come to your barn. After the equine dentist has floated your horse's teeth, you may need to follow up with your equine chiropractor so he can set your horse's TMJ joint (temporomandibular joint). This joint connects the top and bottom jaw and can be shifted out of alignment by dental problems.

Equine dentistry has become quite an art, much more sophisticated than basic floats performed by general practitioners. Plan on spending a fair price for work done with state-of-the-art drills, cutters, and grinders. The skilled work performed by a well-trained equine dentist is worth every penny. Once you are in a heavy training and show program, it will really pay off.

Parasite Control

Regular worming, every two to three months depending on infestation levels, is essential to overall health, well-being, and that perfect show pen appearance. This is one of many situations where you can rely on your veterinarian to suggest what type of wormer to use and at what frequency. If your horse doesn't look quite right, you may want to gather a manure sample and have your veterinarian do a fecal examination to determine possible parasite infestation.

Vaccinations

Vaccination is another area where you can rely on your veterinarian to suggest area-specific treatment. Your veterinarian will also know that when you haul show horses, they can be exposed to a variety of different maladies from horses often brought in from other parts of the country.

Where you will be showing will also factor in to which types of vaccinations you will give. Again, your veterinarian can help you, especially about any area-specific risks.

For example, I gave my horses booster shots last year in June because I heard about an outbreak of flu. I vaccinated them with a booster again in October when we went to the Northwest Quarter Horse Congress among horses from as many as five states and Canada. Respiratory problems can be spread at any show, especially those attracting horses from so many areas. Most adult horses have been exposed to a lot of respiratory infections, but younger horses have not, so it is especially important to give them an influenza booster periodically thoughout the year, every three to six months depending on perceived risk, in addition to their other annual vaccinations. West Nile virus has gained momentum, so I also vaccinate my horses every two to three months for this disease.

Potomac horse fever is one of the problems we don't typically see in the Northwest, nor are public outbreaks of strangles. However, if we were hauling to areas back east where these are more prevalent, we would certainly want our horses vaccinated before the trip.

Plan your vaccination strategy with your veterinarian, who has the networking ability and resources to get updates on outbreaks of disease in both local and distant areas. He can also put your horse on a regular schedule for vaccinations that must be given annually, regardless of whether or not the horses are hauled. These are Eastern and Western encephalomyelitis (and possibly Venezuelan encephalomyelitis, which is area specific), tetanus, and influenza.

Basics for Shoeing Hunter Under Saddle Horses

Shoeing is, of course, specific to the individual horse. But one of my guidelines is that horses should be shod naturally, with their hoof angle matching the angles of the pastern and shoulder.

A hunter under saddle horse should not have excessively long toes, though I do admit that hunt seaters can have a little more toe and longer foot than Western pleasure horses, whose toes are often shortened to produce a shorter stride. In hunt seat we want that greater length of stride. We want the hunter under saddle horse to kick his feet forward, but we don't want them long-toed with no heel, so that they're paddling along as if they were wearing flippers and, therefore, excessively rolling their knees.

Hunter under saddle horses need to have some heel so that they are stood up to the same angle as their pastern and shoulder. Thoroughbreds are tough that way because typically they grow a lot of toe and very little heel, but good shoeing can keep them more upright in the heel, which is easier on their tendons. Shearing off heels causes strain on the check ligaments; stretching and hampering the tendons in the back of the leg risks the possibility of bowed tendons, or pulled suspensory or check ligaments.

During the show season, my horses are shod with aluminum front shoes. They are extremely lightweight, and help promote flat-kneed movement and keep the horses moving with the natural long, low stride we're looking for. The drawback is that aluminum is not as good as steel at absorbing shock. Therefore, while we get wonderful movement by using aluminum shoes, we're risking some joint mobility and comfort. That's why I don't leave them on year round, but shoe in steel during the off season.

During the show season, I often have my shoer put Ultra Lite rim steel shoes on the back feet. The rim's cleat action gives stopping power, which helps keep the hindquarters more stable so the horse has an easier time balancing over his hocks. The downside is that since they really stop the hind feet, there is some degree of jamming in the joints that can cause stifle stress, so I don't use these year round either.

This problem of rim shoes causing soreness in the stifles seems to be more pronounced in longer-backed horses compared to those that are shorter-backed. Also, some horses that don't have ideal conformation, or that have soreness issues in their stifles because of fast growth, seem to do better with a regular flat steel plate behind, even during the show season.

Steel plates, which are a little heavier than the Ultra Lite shoes, come without rims. Whether to use them is a trade-off. You're either going to get the gripping action of the rims which benefits stability, but possibly jeopardize some joints, or use a heavier plate that only slightly jeopardizes movement but is safer on the joints. The answer is to individualize your shoeing program to best fit the needs of your horse.

In the off season, I have the shoer put steel shoes on my horses, all the way around. When I'm not showing, I don't have to worry as much about movement or maintaining flat knees. These months in steel shoes helps save the joints, and this time can be spent healing any injuries or general soreness from athletic wear and tear.

Allowing your horse to go barefoot during the off-show season is definitely recommended if you are not doing a great deal of riding during that time. It toughens the horse's feet and allows them to spread. A great deal of concussion is placed upon a horse's feet with each step. The pressure in pounds per square inch is tremendous, and tiny, narrow feet don't have as much area in which this concussion can be distributed. Even a little spread is beneficial. If you decide to let your horse go barefoot, regular trimming is essential to keep the feet balanced and healthy. Instruct your farrier to cut out the bars but not to take out too much of the sole or frog. A horse needs to develop a thick sole to handle such objects as small rocks. Once he has developed that thick sole, you can barely cut it with a knife. His feet will grow hard as a rock and won't crack.

If you are riding during the winter in snowy climates and your horse is kept in an outside paddock, consider removing his shoes so snow does not pack in the feet. Packed snow, which can become hard as ice, bruises the feet. Staying barefoot lessens that possibility.

If you feel your horse can't go barefoot, shoe the horse with pads and ask your farrier about special shoes that do function in the snow.

Turnout Time

Another aspect of my program that makes it easier on joints is the turnout time I allow my horses. They aren't constantly left in box stalls where their tendons and legs become weak from too little use. I think a lot more lameness issues occur in horses that spend most of their lives confined in stalls. In nature, horses are genetically coded to travel about twenty miles per day. When we stop allowing them to move freely, we risk causing more tendon, leg, and bone problems.

My answer to this is turnout time.

I have a number of large paddocks, some with pasture grass. Most are fenced with ElectroBraid fencing. Weather permitting, I leave the horses out for eight or nine hours on their days off. On training days, they spend at least three hours turned out in their paddocks.

In the summer, the horses wear Sleazy hoods, which cover their heads and necks, and sheets to keep their coats from fading. If it's too hot for a horse to wear these clothes during the heat of the day, they will be fed outside early in the morning, brought into their stalls, and stripped of their clothing at midday, then put back out for a few hours in the late afternoon and evening.

The benefits of turnout time don't stop with tendon, leg, and bone health. Turnout also keeps a horse from getting cranky in his stall and from chewing down the walls. Any horse that is sore, distressed, and cooped up will start exhibiting signs that he's not happy with his life or his job. He may begin pacing, weaving, cribbing, or windsucking in his stall. These are drastic vices that I don't have to deal with because of the outside time I give my horses.

Some of my turnout pens border the outside arena. This was planned, because I believe that horses learn by watching and become less intimidated by the training process when they see other horses performing and enjoying their work. There comes a time when they think, "Hey—I want to be part of that team."

Grooming

Before my horses are saddled, they are groomed with a rubber curry comb to remove dirt, debris, and dead hair, and to bring oils to the surface. Then the job is finished with a soft brush. I don't use a hard brush unless the horse has a thick winter coat.

During warm months, after the horse has been worked and has spent his time tied to the wall or fence, he'll be stripped of the saddle and pad, hosed down with warm water, squeegeed off, and misted with baby or olive oil for coat shine. Rubbing alcohol, instead of oil, can be applied to ease soreness. Spraying Listerine in the cinch area helps prevent fungus.

Many hoof products encourage moisture, but what works best in my barn is WD-40 or mineral oil from a spray bottle. We apply it daily around the coronary band and the outside of the hoof.

Manes and Tails

As long as manes are kept clean—and then not covered with a dirty hood—they are easy to maintain. I'm generally not an advocate of thinning manes. That seems to happen naturally because of braiding. Usually, after the third or fourth show where the mane has been braided, it has become thin enough from hair that is lost in the process. By the end of the show season, we usually wish we had more mane!

Tails are another story. They take a lot of work to keep in condition. My rule of thumb for maintaining long full tails is "Don't comb them!" I'm pretty tough on my clients when I see them going after a tail with a comb. I don't like to comb or brush tails unless they have just been washed and conditioned, and treated with some sort of detangling product. Even then, they still need to be picked through very carefully.

When showing, I enhance the natural tails of my hunter under saddle horses with the use of tail extensions, or "artificial tails." However, the natural tail must be in good condition so that it doesn't present an unhealthy appearance in contrast to the artificial tail. Also, both need to be similar in length and color in order to blend.

Tails can be protected at home with the use of commercial tail bags or homemade devices, but I'm not inclined to use them in the summer months when flies are a problem. There is the possibility the horse will lose more hair by swishing when the tail is braided below the tailbone and put up in a bag, sock, or other protector.

In the winter months, however, I concentrate on heavy conditioning. I saturate a tail from the dock down with a conditioning solution, such as Mane 'n Tail, along with mineral oil. Then, I saturate a pair of panty hose with mineral oil. I start to braid two inches below the tailbone, braiding the panty hose right in with the tail hair. During this process, the excess oil will drip from the tail. Next, I tie up the tail and wrap it with Vetrap, then put it in a tail bag. If the tail is too gooey for the Vetrap to adhere, I use a couple wraps of duct tape over the Vetrap to secure it. This process adds a lot of sheen and glow to the tail. Not only does it provide intense conditioning, it encourages growth. It's not unusual to see six inches of growth in three months.

During this winter conditioning, I don't take the tail down any more frequently than I have to. It might stay tied up for as much as sixty days. If the tail dries out, I just add more mineral oil.

The need for intensive conditioning is area specific. I live in a dry, arid, desertlike environment with very little humidity, so manes, tails, and hooves become quite dry. A person who has a horse in a more humid environment won't need to indulge as often in intense tail and hoof conditioning.

Using "people products" can help with grooming problems. The tops of some tails tend to get fuzzy and stick out. I look for a beauty product called Laminates, made by Sebastian Hair Care

Products. It not only gets the frizz out, but also encourages the upper tail to lie flat.

The Great Cover-Up

Our area gets cold in the winter. The temperature sometimes drops below zero. My winter blanketing program consists of layering as opposed to just one heavyweight blanket. I'll use several blankets that vary from midweight to heavy. Layering adds pockets of air that become warmed; the more layers, the more air pockets, and the more warmth and insulation. This is the system I use for horses that are maintained under stall lights for eighteen hours a day, with six hours of darkness. I use 200 watts of fluorescent lights in the stall, usually on a timer. The key is to have enough wattage in your stalls that you could easily read a newspaper in any corner of the stall. The timers are programmed to turn on the stall lights at 5:00 A.M. and go off at 7:00 A.M. when the horses are turned out into paddocks. The timers again turn on the stall lights at 4:00 P.M., when the horses are returned to the stall for the evening feeding, and turn off at 11:00 P.M. for eighteen hours of total daylight. A horse kept under lights will become slick-haired, either shedding out a long winter coat early, or just not growing it in the first place because of the "long days" the lights produce. The brain is tricked into thinking it's spring. If you are planning to attend winter shows and want your horse slick, a light program and blankets are a necessity.

Horses that are truly on their off season in the winter, with no light program and sporting a full winter coat, are better off *not* being blanketed. A horse's coat is designed to stand up when it's cold so air between hair follicles is trapped and warmed. When we put blankets on furry horses, they mat the hair down. That takes away the horse's ability to capture and warm air between the follicles. We've totally eliminated any sort of natural insulation.

A blanket and hood regimen needs constant management. Never leave hoods on your horse for days without checking underneath.

Turnout time is an important part of my program. My grass paddocks have ElectroBraid fencing. This horse has on a Sleazy hood and sheet to keep the sun from bleaching his coat.

He might lose his mane. You should also remove blankets regularly. Leaving them on for long periods of time can leave devastating marks, much like the indentations made on a person's ring finger. It becomes even worse with blankets that don't fit well. They will rub hair off the horse's shoulders near the chest, which leaves bald spots. If they rub or put a lot of pressure on the horse's withers, a pressure sore will develop. These often "hair in," similar to saddle sores, with white hair, regardless of the base color of the horse, making them extremely obvious.

It's also vital that Lycra Sleazy hoods fit well. If they don't, the elastic nosebands can leave permanent scars on the bridge of the horse's nose, again making it possible for hair to grow in white in that area.

It's a Lot of Work

Properly managing a show horse puts big demands on your time, but there is nothing more rewarding than knowing you did a good job and that your horse is healthy, happy, sound, and fit.

EQUINE BODY SCORE

- **Score of 1—Poor:** This animal has no fatty tissue that can be felt. His skeletal features are easily seen, including ribs, hip joints, and lower pelvic bones.
- **Score of 2—Very Thin:** There is only a slight covering of fat on this horse. In general, he is emaciated, but is not as bad as a "Score 1" horse.
- **Score of 3—Thin:** While this horse's ribs will be "covered" with a slight amount of fat and are not as easily seen as with the above two horses, they can still be felt.
- **Score of 4—Moderately Thin:** Race, endurance, and polo horses might be fine when in this condition. They are fit and generally healthy at this weight. Excess weight would cause a lot of stress on their legs, given their jobs. They look "fit,"

but not as obviously thin as horses with the above three scores.

- **Score of 5—Moderate:** This is a good, general score for most horses, including your hunter under saddle horse. He will have enough fat on his back that his spine doesn't appear to protrude. His tailhead won't protrude. His body in general looks "well covered," with just enough fat.
- **Score of 6—Moderately Fleshy:** This is still within a range that I would consider fine for most horses, including the hunter under saddle horse with a larger frame or bigger bone. He has a little more fat than the Score 5 horse. He might have a slight crease down his back, and he has enough fat covering his ribs that the area feels a little spongy. His withers don't protrude and his shoulders are well covered.
- **Score of 7—Fleshy:** Starting with this score, a horse is a little too fleshy for what I'd consider the ideal hunter under saddle look. He is starting to develop fat on his withers and his neck.
- **Score of 8—Fat:** This horse has a definite crease down his back. His withers are fleshy and some thickness has formed on his neck and inner thighs. Not good for a hunter under saddle horse.
- **Score of 9—Extremely Fat:** Bulging fat is appearing on this horse, over his ribs and withers and along his neck. This is your basic "plus-sized" horse.

4

DECISIONS ON TACK

◄◦►

Choice of tack will have a strong influence on how successful you are with your training program.

Starting Safe

I start my hunter under saddle horses in a lightweight, beat-up western work saddle. They can hit it against the round corral wall or reach around and chew on it, and it's no big deal. This "toss-around" saddle is safe for both horse and rider. The billets, girth, and fenders are in good condition, so there is no chance of breaking. The tree is sound, and the saddle fits the horse, with some daylight between the high withers of a specialized Thoroughbred horse and the saddle's gullet (the space under the pommel). A horse can almost be crippled with a bad saddle that pinches the withers or the loin area.

Another aspect of rider safety is also a big factor in my decision to use a western saddle through the first few months of riding. None of us wants to be thrown like a Frisbee from the back of a 16.2 two-year-old, or for that matter, a horse of any age or size. Using the western saddle for training allows the rider to be more secure and have better balance. In turn, this promotes balance and coordination in the young horse.

Start With the Basic Snaffle and Go From There

If a colt is light (very responsive to light pressure from the bit) and wants to remain soft and supple in his mouth, I start him in a smooth snaffle bit and keep him in it for quite a while. You will read when and why I change from the snaffle, but in the beginning this is a good bit to use on a young horse, especially *before* starting to work on a headset.

Two important fundamentals here are that: (1) Snaffles are designed to lift and elevate the head. This is an advantage, because when we start teaching a young horse to elevate his shoulders, he will need to keep his head up in order to achieve that elevation. Snaffle bits also promote lateral movement of the head due to the direct contact with the horse's lips, bars (the area between incisors and canines in males or the premolars in females), and tongue area. (2) Curb bits are designed to lower and drop the head and neck, by using leverage from the shanks and applying mouth pressure to either or all of these parts in the horse's mouth: the bars, tongue, roof of mouth, and under the chin area where the chinstrap lies.

Snaffle bits are great for lateral work, to teach a horse to bend his body in the direction in which his head is moving. Here, however, many riders become confused. They leave their horses in a snaffle bit far too long and end up dulling the very mouth they're trying to lighten. Using a snaffle doesn't automatically mean your horse will have a light, responsive mouth, although it is a good tool to use in starting a horse. However, the minute he starts rooting and pushing against the bit, shoving his nose forward or down in an attempt to take the bit away from your hands, you should step him up into a twisted wire snaffle or some type of leverage curb bit with a broken mouthpiece to get respect back.

A leverage bit differs from a snaffle in that it has shanks and a chinstrap. The mouthpiece can either be broken, like a snaffle, or solid. I will use a broken-mouthpiece curb bit for one to three days, depending on the response from the horse. If he stays relaxed in his neck and respectful in his mouth, I will continue to use the leverage bit. But if he begins to overflex—if he brings his chin in toward his chest as though he's trying to back away from the bit, I can see that he is intimidated. I will then go back to the snaffle since he has learned a lesson about not being "heavy" in the mouth. I want him to become lighter in the mouth and more respectful of my hands, but I do not want him to become intimidated by the bit.

I might use a variety of bits on a young horse. It is important to find the right balance. I may change between a snaffle and a shank snaffle depending on the clues I am getting from my horse. When he gets heavy in my hands with the snaffle, I will begin using the shank snaffle for added leverage. Once the horse lightens in the mouth or begins to exhibit signs of intimidation, I will go back to the smooth or twisted wire snaffle. Varying bits keeps him from becoming dull-mouthed. I want to convey this message: "Look, I'm still in charge here. You cannot run through my hands."

A twisted wire can be used to encourage a horse to be more responsive, especially to correct a horse that wants to pull your arms out of the sockets. But this more severe bit has to be used with extreme caution. You won't have to muscle him around with extreme force. If it is too sharp a wire and you use it with a heavy hand, you'll intimidate a horse to the extent that he won't stretch his neck out in a relaxed manner and carry the bit as desired. He'll become rigid in his neck and tense his shoulders and will carry his head back too far, tucked behind the vertical. By not wanting to drop forward and relax his head and neck, he loses the relaxed length of neck you're trying to encourage. Extremes in choosing and using curb bits can produce the same unwanted results. The more sucked back the horse is behind the vertical, the shorter his stride will be. Horses typically will only stretch their front legs out to where their nose is, because their vision does not allow them to see their front feet, so they will not step beyond a point to which their noses have already traveled.

After correcting a horse with a leverage bit or twisted wire snaffle, step him back down to a less severe bit. You've told him, "I want your respect. As long as you're soft in your mouth, I'll be soft in my hands." Now, he should surf his neck out and keep his head and mouth quiet. He won't push through the bridle or root at the bit. He'll just lie there softly in your hands and reach for the bridle.

Your horse needs light contact to help him balance as he learns to travel in self-carriage. If he's moving correctly from behind, using his haunches to drive up underneath his belly and propel himself, your light bridle contact helps him balance his neck and drop into the bridle.

This is the desired frame you'll want in the hunter under saddle show pen. By keeping this picture in mind as your ultimate goal, you can use different leverage bits to produce a soft mouth. Then, on show day, you can successfully use a snaffle and convey the message to the judge that shows how light and supple your horse is in this mild bit.

Draw Reins and Martingales

Especially during those first few months under saddle, I don't like to use draw reins or martingales on a horse. If I do use them, it's only for a day or two. Used for extended periods of time, draw reins and martingales have a tendency to overdevelop the top neck muscles because of the overflexed position that occurs at the poll.

If you find yourself resorting to this type of equipment during the early stages of training you're probably doing it to gain leverage. The quest for leverage could better be addressed by using a curb bit with a broken mouthpiece, and leaving the draw reins or martingale in the tack room.

Later in the training process a martingale can occasionally be used in obtaining a headset that is more consistent and at a desired level. But a martingale should never be used constantly, nor should it be used with force (more about this in the chapter on finishing work and headsets). We're not looking for that "accordion" appearance in a horse's head and neck caused by misuse of draw reins and martingales. People get in a hurry to work on a headset, but it is the last thing on my mind during those first few months. I'm an advocate of teaching the hunter under saddle horse to move with a long, stretched-out neck. I want a horse's front feet to extend clear out under his nose, reaching far forward with every stride. If you break that up, you lose the stride in front. He'll stiffen his shoulders, which immediately causes him to lose fluidity and length of stride. The horse will travel in a short-stepping, choppy manner with his front end. He'll land quickly instead of floating. He'll look like a jackhammer with hair.

It's hard to get a horse away from that type of movement once gimmicks have been overused.

Moving Into the Hunt Saddle

The decision of when to switch your horse to the English hunt saddle is purely up to you. Factors include how you feel about your balance, how much experience you have had in an English saddle, and your horse's progress. Although this subject will be addressed more fully later in the book, just remember now that there is no hurry in switching your horse to the hunt saddle during his preshow training. If you have had little experience riding in a hunt saddle, you may need to consider riding a well-trained English horse to fine-tune your hunt-seat riding skills before schooling your young horse in the hunt saddle for the first time.

It is not atypical of a hunt-seat prospect to require a little more warm-up time when you first start using a hunt saddle. The hunt saddle will have different pressure points, and the horse will need to become accustomed to the new feel. The more sensitive the horse, the longer it will take him to adjust.

A well-fitted saddle shouldn't feel uncomfortable to a horse, but will rest on him in different ways from the western saddle. It is not

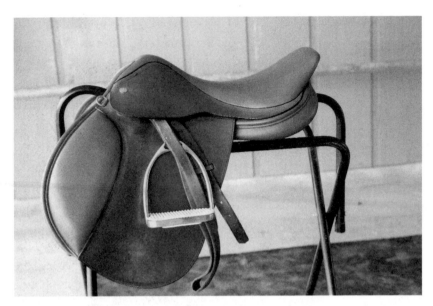

When to switch your horse to an English hunt saddle is purely up to you. The decision should be based on how safe and balanced you feel in such tack, as well as your horse's progress.

uncommon for a hunter under saddle prospect to overly round his back when first introduced to a well-fitted hunt saddle. They need a little time to realize something is different. But, within a few minutes on the longe line, they will relax and become accepting of the "new saddle."

If your usually good-natured horse pins his ears, switches his tail, violently throws his head down, and tries to buck you off, you might have a saddle problem. He might refuse to go forward, and sink to the pressure and almost sway his back. He might string his body out and trail his hocks behind. All are signs that a saddle isn't fitting him properly.

Hunt saddles produced years ago were made with a narrower spine that fit right over the thoracic vertebrae of the horse. That's where horses felt the pain. Saddle makers today are improving their products by making them quite a bit wider through the spine. They

Today's hunt saddles, which are wide through the spine, sit comfortably on the horse. It's easy to slip four fingers in the spine, whereas with older saddles you'll be lucky to fit two fingers in that area. Such narrow spines are not as comfortable for a horse.

now fit much like the tree of a western saddle and sit down on the horse. When you turn over a newer hunt saddle to inspect it, you can easily get four fingers down the spine. With older saddles, you'd be lucky to fit two fingers in that area.

Bits for Reschooling the Older Horse

If you're working with an older horse that needs to go back to basics, you will be facing one of two evils. Either the horse is lazy and doesn't want to move forward, or he's traveling too fast and taking control of the bridle, leaving the rider totally behind.

With a horse that's trying to run off, you might do well using a correctional bit with a shank, or a Kimberwicke with a correctional mouthpiece in your training program. The correction bit is designed with a port, to add palate pressure as well as pressure on the bars (the gum area between the front and back teeth), for more leverage. Its broken mouthpiece adds suppling and lateral movement. This bit, which should only be used by a horseman who is soft-handed and who rides with a high degree of balance, will help back the horse off the bridle and reestablish respect. It will also redistribute the horse's weight to lift his shoulders and rock back on his haunches. You can then start work on softening his neck, executing lateral moves, and encouraging him to relax through his shoulders and stretch out his neck.

After lightening up a horse's mouth with a correction bit, go back to a Kimberwicke with a snaffle mouth to encourage neck elongation.

As a rule, an older lazy horse can go into a basic slow twist snaffle for schooling. If he's a little heavy in hand, remember that he can always move back into a twisted wire snaffle or a Kimberwicke. If you are sure this horse is just lazy and not sore from age and arthritis, use a crop to encourage him to loosen up and stride forward when schooling him at home. He'll also need a lot of cross-over shoulder exercises, explained later in this book, to help him start extending his front legs out in front of him, building his stride, and pushing off with impulsion from his hindquarters.

Tack for the Show Pen

Whether performing with a younger or older horse, there's nothing wrong with showing in the hunter under saddle event in a Kimberwicke or even a pelham. The pelham, which combines elements of both a snaffle and a curb bit, is not seen very often at breed shows. This bit has lost its appeal because it is difficult not to overbridle a horse and cause stiffness in the neck.

The Kimberwicke is a nice choice that has replaced the pelham bit for many riders. It operates as either a leverage bit or a snaffle, depending on how it is attached to the reins. The top rein slot operates like a snaffle. The bottom rein slot acts like a curb bit with leverage action. Whenever a fixed-rein attachment is use—which means the rein does not move freely around the bit ring, but rather attaches to a slot on the ring—a chinstrap at least one-half inch in width is required by most breed show rulebooks. The chinstrap must lie flat against the area under the horse's chin.

Your horse's mouth will tell you which of these two settings to use, or even if a different type of mouthpiece is necessary. Use a snaffle-type mouthpiece for the horse that needs just a little leverage. Or, go all the way up to a correctional mouthpiece with a little more tongue relief. A Kimberwicke has a very short shank without excessive leverage; it can really encourage a horse to surf out his neck and drop down into the bridle. It is a light-leverage bit where a smooth-ring snaffle is a non-leverage bit.

I hear a lot of people say, "I'm working with a young rider on an older horse and I don't want him to hurt the horse's mouth, so we'll put the horse in a smooth ring snaffle." That's like putting the rider in a car that is going a hundred miles per hour and taking away the brake pedal. The only way the youngster is strong enough to get the horse stopped is to "put his foot through the floorboards." Pushing his feet forward this way sacrifices the rider's balance and equitation ability. Putting this horse in a leverage bit will convince the horse to respect the child, while also teaching the child to ride with soft hands when given proper instruction.

Know Your Bit Details

Bits are an important piece of the puzzle in training horses. You will need a clear understanding of their design and function. If your horse is hard to control or stop, you'll need a bit with more leverage. If he throws his head up every time you pull on him, investigate the problem. Maybe you need to use your hands in a softer, smoother, and quieter manner. You might also need to go back to a softer bit with less leverage, or ask an equine dentist for an exam.

BIT TERMS

- **Broken mouthpiece:** A mouthpiece that is hinged in the center, usually with one to two hinged joints.
- **Leverage:** Curb bits produce leverage, and the curb strap and the mouthpiece apply pressure on areas in and around

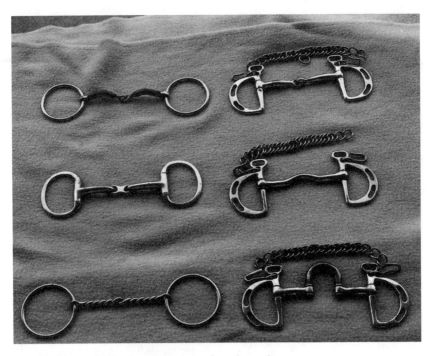

Snaffle bits and Kimberwickes in order of severity.

[On the left, in descending order]

- *Ring snaffle – mild. I start my young horses in them.*
- *Snaffle with jointed mouthpiece – a step up from "mild."*
- *Twisted wire snaffle – more severe, and therefore extreme care is required.*

[on the right, in descending order]

- *Kimberwicke with a snaffle mouthpiece – mild.*
- *Kimberwicke with a solid mouthpiece – a step up from "mild."*
- *Kimberwicke with a correctional mouthpiece – more severe than the other two Kimberwickes.*

Kimberwicke with the reins adjusted in the bottom slot. Using this bit applies pressure in the mouth and on the chin (from the chain) much like a shank bit. For use with an older horse.

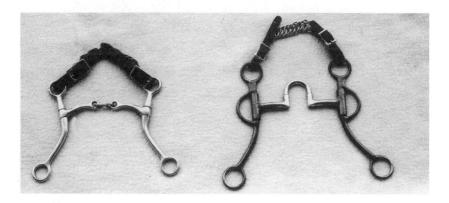

Shank bits:

Left – a jointed mouth shank snaffle offers enough leverage to encourage a young horse that is heavy in the bit to lighten up.

Right – Correctional bit for use on older, more broke horses that need to be lightened up.

the horse's mouth. This could be on the bars, lips, soft palate, or tongue. Shank length determines the amount of leverage—the longer the shank, the more leverage.

- **Correctional Bit:** Designed with good balance to promote feel in the horse's mouth. They are generally used on older horses to fix problems rather than for constant use. This advanced bit should only be used by an advanced and well-balanced rider.

5

PERSONAL SPACE AND FOLLOW-THE-LEADER

◄◦►

If you don't have respect from a horse when you're on the ground, you won't get it from the saddle. My personal space exercise and the follow-the-leader routine initiate the environment necessary to gain respect. It is all based on herd behavior.

Let's look what happens out in the pasture. The herd's boss mare walks on a narrow path. Other horses follow behind her. If one of them tailgates, she throws herself in reverse and lets fly with both back legs, kicking the horse behind her in the chest. Even though the boss mare never turns her head around to look at him directly, the tailgater will back off.

The young horse quickly learns to read the body language of the boss mare in order to get behavioral directions.

In my training program, I take on the leadership role as the herd's boss mare, and therefore encourage the young horse to take instruction from me through my body language, which says, "Look to me for your instructions because I'm the boss."

Of course, I don't double-hock kick my horse, but like the four-legged herd mare, I keep the horse behind me and keep my back to him.

This schooling can start with weanlings or yearlings, but I don't put a timeline on it. I start working on personal space the minute a horse starts impeding on it, no matter how old he is. If I lead a horse out of the barn and he tries to walk over me or tap dance on my toes, then I take care of that problem immediately, because he is being disrespectful and fighting for my hierarchy. He needs to learn to stay back and respect my space.

I don't usually introduce the follow-the-leader routine, however, until I have my horses leading well and longeing. This is usually when they're long yearlings or coming two-year-olds and I'm getting serious about starting their round pen work and, later, riding them.

Don't Tread On Me

I use a long cotton lead rope for teaching personal space and follow-the-leader. Sometimes I use a chain over the horse's nose. Other times I don't, determined by how sensitive the horse is to discipline. If he is "numb" and doesn't respond to a halter and lead rope, I will use the chain.

I walk off, leading the horse on a loose line behind me. I am not leading from the traditional leading position as seen in a showmanship or halter class. I give him about ten feet of slack so he can assume a position six to eight feet behind me. If he tries to walk over or past me, I stop him and back him up, either with pressure on the chain or the rope or by slapping him on the chest with the leadrope. My back stays to him, so he's learning from the start to duplicate my movements.

When I start walking again, the horse starts to realize that he needs to give me a head start, about eight feet of space. When the slack is out of the rope, I will cluck to him with my voice and nudge him along by tugging on the rope so he'll start to follow. When I stop, he is to stop. When I back up (with my back to him), he is to step back. We end up doing a dance of movement, only he's responding from eight to ten feet away. When done correctly, it becomes a great exhibition of personal space.

I walk off with a lot of slack. The horse is about ten feet behind me.

The handler has to hold a posture and attitude that exhibit confidence. You must walk with purpose. You need to walk faster than a saunter, because when you hit the brakes and stop, the suddenness of your halt should, in a sense, spook the horse into backing. Using quick, snappy movements earns the attention and respect desired. Nagging a horse doesn't work. He'll just tune you out. Again, putting it in a herd context, the boss mare doesn't slowly come to a stop, ease back, and quietly say "beep, beep" as a warning. She disciplines the tailgating horse behind her, and she does it quickly, and then continues walking down the path.

If your horse is paying attention and moves back when you stop and back up towards him, reward him immediately by turning and petting him on the forehead.

This schooling comes in handy in many ways, such as when an assistant is needed to work through an issue with a horse. For example, if I'm ground driving a horse in the round pen and trying to

I stop quickly and "spook" the horse so that he moves back.

When he responds correctly, I pat him on the forehead as a reward.

back him up, and he doesn't want to step back to my hand pressure from the lines, I have an assistant stand in front of the horse with his back to the horse's head. I'll drive the horse so that he follows the assistant for a short time. Then the assistant will stop. As I pull back with the driving lines, my assistant backs up toward the horse in the same way as I did when I was leading, stopped, and "spooked" the horse back. Even though the ground driving is new to the horse, the follow-the-leader routine is not, and the horse gains confidence from our reverting to something he's already learned.

A big part of my program is building off of the basics and, when necessary, returning to a foundation basic that the horse knows well. His training keeps building on itself in a very systematic way. Nothing comes out of the blue.

If something completely foreign is presented to a horse, and he just doesn't get it, some people start doing things to the horse that they shouldn't. The person overdisciplines the horse out of his or her own frustration. A brawl ensues, and there is no communication. This sort of situation does not need to happen.

When communicating in a language your horse understands, training goals are realized much faster. You'll be amazed at how easy training is if handled by building a strong foundation using personal space and follow-the-leader work as a starting point.

6

ROUND PEN BASICS

————◄○►————

A young horse is taught several basics in a round pen so that by the time he graduates to the big training arena, his rider will have both confidence and control. Some very important lessons are introduced during this work, starting with understanding the meaning of voice commands and most importantly the word "Whoa." The horse also learns to move his shoulders and hips, give to the bridle, and accept the weight of the saddle. This all leads to the first few rides under saddle, which are done in the round pen.

I strongly recommend the use of a round pen that is at least fifty feet in diameter, with sixty feet actually being the optimum size. This gives the advantage of a smaller space in controlling the horse and easily encourages him to move forward as he learns to longe; but it's not so small that there is a high risk of stress on the horse's joints.

Before working a horse in the round pen, I put protective leg gear on the front legs, such as splint boots and bell boots, because a young horse is fairly uncoordinated at this stage and is liable to interfere, which is hitting one front leg or hoof with the other. There is also the risk of the horse developing a splint due to the tight size of a small round pen.

More Philosophy

From the moment I start working with a young horse, I don't treat him like a baby. I don't sneak around tiptoeing, afraid of causing a ruckus. The use of the walking-on-eggs method creates cautious and timid behavior in the young horse. If you exhibit fear, he too will be fearful, but if you exhibit confidence in your actions, your colt will gain confidence from you.

I keep the bigger picture in mind. I set the horse up to learn a lot of things by himself. I casually go about what I need to do, and don't react if the horse spooks. I keep my expectations in line with the age of the horse. However, I treat a young horse the same way I treat my older horses, being sure to leave the baby voice out of my learning sessions. If you treat a young horse like a two-year-old forever, he will forever act like a two-year-old.

Voice Commands

This is an appropriate time to determine what voice commands you want to have in your training program. I use different voice commands for different maneuvers. For instance, I will use one cluck to encourage my horse to walk, repetitive clucks for the trot, a kissing sound for the canter, the verbal "whoa" for the stop, and a soft ticking sound, by snapping my tongue against my clenched teeth, for the back. I prefer to use these types of sounds instead of conversational speech of "walk," "trot," "canter," and "back" because I feel it is easier for the horse to distinguish sounds and tones as opposed to words. However, as long as you are consistent in your cues, use whatever is most comfortable.

Shoulders 101

Since teaching a horse to use his shoulders is a primary part of my training program, I use the round pen to introduce the concept. In the personal space and follow-the-leader work, I taught the horse to trail behind me and move in response to my movements. I take this one step further in the round corral. I walk toward the horse's shoulder and cluck, asking him for a turn on the haunches. As I step in, I want him to move his shoulders away from my body, crossing his front leg nearest me across and in front of the other front leg. If he doesn't, I lightly slap his shoulder with my hand or the lead rope to help him understand what I'm after. If he resists and moves into me, I become more assertive with my discipline, making sure to convey a message to remind him of my hierarchy and personal space. In most cases, he will then readily move his shoulders.

This is the foundation I want to establish from the start. Why? Because a horse moves from its shoulders. He can actually turn his head in one direction, but move in the other. However, it is where the horse's shoulders are moving that determines his direction of travel.

Round pen work also gives a young horse the basics of responding to direct-rein pressure. Many people are confused about the reasons for tying a horse's head around (explained later in this chapter) to teach him to "follow his nose." Yes, we're trying to teach him to bend and move into the direction that his head is cocked, but there's an ultimate goal above and beyond that. We want his shoulders to follow his nose, the start of gaining control over the shoulders.

To teach the horse to move his shoulders, I begin by walking toward his shoulder as if asking for a showmanship turn.

I want him to move his shoulders away from me. If he doesn't respond, I tap his shoulder with my hand or the lead rope.

I can also walk toward a young horse's hip in the round corral and teach him to move his hindquarters away from me (turn on the forehand), using the same technique used to move his shoulders.

All this work leads to the type of body control that is necessary for a hunter under saddle horse to be successful in the show pen. Beginning in the round pen and using exercises with consistent cues, followed by appropriately delivered praise and corrections, will establish a positive training foundation on which to build a horse's education fundamentals.

Longe Line Workdays One Through Three

After the horse fully understands the personal space and follow-the-leader exercises, I teach him to longe in the round pen. The horse has learned to cue and move off my body with the follow-the-leader work, so he'll do the same when the longe line goes on.

I do very little off the lead rope. Most of what I do to stop or move the horse is accomplished with the movement of my body in and out of his flight zone.

Using the same method, I teach the horse to move his hip away from me.

The diagram below illustrates this flight zone. The front of the flight zone is at the horse's eye; the back of the zone is at his tail. A triangle is formed with the narrow side in the area of the pen where I'm standing and the wide section at the horse's eye and tail.

I can remain in the middle of the pen, or move a little closer to the horse by walking in a small circle. To drive him forward off my body movement, I step behind the back of his flight zone. In other words, if he's traveling to the left, I step to the right until I am in a line behind the right point of the widest side of the triangle, past his hip.

Do not stand directly behind the horse, but remain a safe distance away. Using your body in and out of the flight zone to move your horse does not mean that you stay so close that the horse could kick or strike you.

If I want the horse to slow down, I step ahead of the imaginary triangle line that extends to his shoulder. If I want him to stop and turn, I move forward to a point off of his eye.

Using this flight zone correctly teaches the horse to go forward, to halt, and to turn and go in the other direction, all by using the

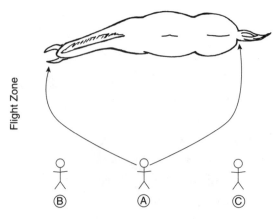

Flight zone: a horse's flight zone extends from his eye (B) to his tail (C). In a normal longeing position, I will be positioned at (A), which is the point of the imaginary triangle. If I want to move him forward or increase his speed, I step back to the "C" area. If I want him to slow down, or stop, I move to the "B" area.

horse's own language—the same cues that would cause him to move away from another horse in the herd.

The amount of longeing I do the first day depends on how the horse responds. I am always concerned about not stressing his legs, so I want to do only the amount of longeing that is absolutely necessary to accomplish the lesson plan for that day. Making a horse go around and around forever without a purpose will not only dull him from learning, but would risk potential injury to his legs. If my goal is to teach a horse to longe for the first time, I try to get all that information to him in a twenty-minute session. I don't like to overwork the horse at the trot or canter the first few times, always remembering that this is a young horse's beginning work in the circle. His tendons and ligaments have to adjust and gradually become conditioned. If I can get the horse to travel to the left at the trot and canter, make him stop, reverse, then trot and canter to the right, his first lesson in longeing is complete.

However, if a horse continually wants to stop and face me, I use the longe whip to encourage him to get out of my personal space and back toward the rail. The amount of force used with the whip depends upon how resistant the horse is to moving out of my space. I use no more whip than I have to, given the circumstances. The longe whip, an extension of my hand, requests respect. I don't use it to instill fear into a youngster. If a person picks up a whip and the horse flees for his life, the longe whip has been misused, and lessons are needed to desensitize the horse to the whip.

Such desensitizing takes patience. First, stand the horse in the middle of the round pen. Double the whip over, so that you are holding the handle and the end of the whiptail in one hand. Touch the horse all over with the whip. Then, let go of the whiptail and swing the whip around the horse. This is not a Wild West show whip-cracking event, but just easy swinging. Be very careful not to hit the horse's face. When the horse becomes quiet and stands as the swinging whip gently touches him, slap the ground with the whip, or tap his body to encourage him to return to the rail and move forward. Then continue with the longeing lessons.

I swing the whip a lot when the horse is longeing. I don't hit or scare him, I just continue the desensitizing process so the horse gains confidence in my instruction and doesn't fear the whip. One of my Jack Russell terriers often comes into the round pen. He loves to jump the longe line, chase the whip, and hang from the whiptail. It is amazing how this commotion desensitizes a horse. Even though the dog is being silly, he doesn't interfere with the horse. On the contrary, by chasing the whip, he's teaching the young horse not to react to flying objects or dogs that lurk along the horse show rail. In fact, the horse becomes more interested in watching the antics of the dog than in being afraid of the whip. He still respects it as an extension of my arm, though, and it's there if needed for any type of correction.

I don't abuse a horse with a whip, nor do I nag. I use a "three strikes and you're out" system. I ask softly with a voice command. If the horse doesn't do what I ask, I don't discipline at that point. After I ask, I tell with a command that is more firm. Then, if he doesn't do what I ask, I discipline, but I don't overdo.

For instance, if I want a horse to go from a trot to a canter, I give my voice command for this transition, which is a kissing sound. This is the "ask." If I don't get a canter response, again, I kiss at the horse, but this time I also hold up the whip. This is the "tell." If the horse still doesn't go into the canter, I kiss and snap the whip behind the horse, or actually touch him with the whip—the "discipline."

The exception to the "three strikes" approach is when a horse kicks out at me. I don't tolerate that misbehavior. I'll use the whip once, below the hock, the instant he kicks. It is a sensitive area, and I'm sure to get his attention. I'm careful not to injure the horse, but at the same time I need to relay a strong message of intolerance towards this offensive and dangerous behavior.

A horse that kicks out, wrings his tail, or pins his ears perceives himself as higher in the hierarchy. He is challenging you for his status. He is typically a more aggressive and dominant horse that needs a more aggressive reaction from you to keep him respecting you and your training. This aggressive attitude must be nipped in the bud immediately, or the disrespect will continue when you start to ride him.

Whoa

When I begin teaching the horse to stop on the longe line, I step in front of his flight space. My commands come from my body and my voice more than from my hand. If a horse doesn't stop, I will try one more time by stepping harder and faster in front of that flight space, lifting my whip in front of the horse. I only use pressure on the lead rope if it becomes apparent that the horse is ignoring my body position and planning on running past me. Once again, I stress the three strikes approach—ask, tell, demand.

Working with the horse's flight space creates in him a mental picture of what is expected. Before long he is really in tune to my movements and my voice.

Saddling Up

I'm not a fan of snubbing a horse (holding him with a strong grip at the halter) during the initial saddling process because this generally causes fear to resonate in the animal. When a young horse has a quiet and amiable disposition, I will saddle him without the help of an assistant. However, I believe that having someone to aid in this process is extremely beneficial and I solicit help whenever possible.

For my own safety, if I am working with a horse I don't know well, or one that is flighty by nature, I would definitely have an assistant help me during that first saddling session. This person stands at the horse's head, but there is no hanging on tightly to the halter. I want the horse to stand with two feet of free rope and a relaxed demeanor.

On the first day that I decide to saddle, I use the round pen's top rail as a saddle rack. I place both the saddle and pad on the fence, then longe the horse around the pen in each direction. He might look at these foreign objects and spook. I don't worry if he does. I just keep longeing until he relaxes.

On the day I plan to saddle the horse for the first time, I use the round pen's top rail as a saddle rack for both the saddle and the pad. Being longed past them in both directions helps him become accustomed to the tack.

After longeing, I'll have my handler stand on the inside of the round pen near the rail and hold the horse facing, but not touching, the fence to inhibit extreme forward motion. I won't restrain a small amount of movement. I don't want him to feel claustrophobic or be put into a situation that will make him feel trapped. That would create fear and hinder a proper environment for learning.

I will pull the pad down and let the horse sniff it. I touch him all over with the pad on one side, then walk around the front and repeat the process on the other side. I just lightly hit him with the pad on the belly, the legs, behind his hip—all over. Then, I hand the pad to my assistant while I get the saddle down from the fence.

Let me stress that at this stage I do not want the saddle or pad to fall off the horse. If the horse starts to buck, I pull off the saddle or pad, or both. But to let the horse dump them on the ground means I have lost control of the equipment, and the horse is set up for a learned behavior. He thinks, "Ah-ha! Bucking equals exodus, and this stuff is off my back!" This is not at all what I want the horse to think.

I use a lightweight saddle that is easy to toss around. I put the cinch over the top of the saddle and secure the right stirrup over the saddle horn. I show the saddle to the horse. He'll sniff it. Then I toss it and rattle it on both sides of him. When he is calm about this introduction, I set the pad and then the saddle up on his back.

If I don't get the saddle in the proper position the first time, I start again. I pull the gear off and if the horse moves away from me, I don't chase him with the saddle. I don't force the issue. Even if I do get the saddle where I want it, if the horse moves, I might pull it right off his back and start the process over, as many times as it takes for him to stand still and be relaxed.

Only if everything goes right, the saddle is in place, and the horse is comfortable and quiet, do I cinch him up. I want the cinch tight enough to withstand a bit of bucking or a run-off, but not so tight that it makes the horse uncomfortable. To do so at this point could create the vice of the horse being cinchy, which would mean that he

When I've allowed the horse to smell and investigate the saddle and he is calm, I'll set the pad and saddle on his back.

would pin his ears, bite at the handler, or stomp his feet in protest at being cinched. Horses have a tendency to hold their breath when being saddled, which causes the cinch to loosen when the horse begins to breathe normally again, so I check the cinch periodically throughout the lesson time to insure that it remains snug.

Once the cinch is tightened and secure, I take the horse's longe line from my assistant and ask him or her to leave the pen. I then walk the horse to the center of the round pen so I'm not trapped between the horse and the wall. I lead the horse in a normal leading style, standing near his head, rather than having him walk several feet behind me as I did in the follow-the-leader work. We walk in a five-meter circle, with me positioned inside the center of the circle.

Should the horse become upset, I have enough control over his head so he can't strike at or jump into me. If he tries, I send him in a circle around me. I don't react if he gets excited. It's better not to make a big issue out of it. If I stay calm, the horse thinks, "Gee, I'm acting like an idiot, but she isn't so maybe there's nothing to be afraid of." I look for signs from the horse to tell me he is relaxing and becoming quiet and comfortable. He might cock an ear toward me. He might chew or lower his head and neck. These are all signs he is yielding to my authority and is looking to me for instructions.

The biggest thing my clients and I will discuss about working with a young horse is my philosophy on not reacting. I don't react if a horse spooks or pitches a fit. If you have the edge on the hierarchy between you and a young horse, and you stay calm, cool, and relaxed, he should calm down and cause very little problem. However, if he gets you into a dither and you fall prey to his game, this behavior will happen again and again. So, if a horse goes ballistic with the saddle, don't sweat it. You've already taught him to longe. Just keep him on a very short line, moving around you, and let him get his ya-yas out. He'll start to relax, and when he does, give him some slack and let him move to the full space of the round corral as he longes.

After the horse works during this first week, I take him out of the round corral and tie him to the solid wall at the end of my arena. I

If everything goes right, I can cinch him up tight enough to keep the saddle in place if he bucks or runs off, but not so tight that it would be uncomfortable.

leave him there. If he stands quietly, I untie him fifteen to thirty minutes later. If he is pawing and acting hyper, I wait until he quiets down. In the beginning, the horse is in control of how much time he spends tied there. He figures out that standing quietly at the wall means the stay is shorter, but throwing a fit means a longer stint at

I longe him with the saddle.

the wall. At first, that "longer stint" is rarely more than thirty minutes. It is important, though, that the horse not be retrieved if he is behaving badly. The retrieval is thus the reward for good behavior.

I want to stress the importance of tying to an extremely safe fence. Mine, a high plywood wall secured with railroad ties that are sunk deep into the ground, is really safe because there is nothing for a horse to put his legs through or jump into. Building this type of structure is inexpensive insurance to keep a horse injury free.

If there is any chance that a horse will pull back, I tie him with either a bungee cord rope or an inner tube that is secured to the post. This way, if he tries in any way to test the line, he never meets up with solid pressure. The bungee or inner tube will bounce him forward into the pressure release of the tie. This is an extremely good practice to use on a young horse that is just learning to be tied, because it prevents the vice of pulling back. He soon learns that he might as well just stand still and not raise a fuss.

As my training program continues, the young horse's time on the wall increases in order to promote patience. A horse will quickly learn to relax and even sleep. I often have five or six other horses tied around the arena. They enjoy each other's company and seem to like being part of the team.

During the time the young horse is first tied, there's a chance he'll rub the saddle against the wall or reach around to chew on a stirrup. That's why I don't use a show saddle for this work. Rubbing or chewing an old beat-up saddle is not a big deal. And if you don't raise a fuss, 90 percent of the time the problem will disappear on its own.

When the weather is cold, I put a blanket or cooler over the saddle to keep the horse from getting chilled. It's not unusual to see a young horse playing with the ties on a cooler or even pulling it off. Again—I don't make a big deal out of it.

Introducing the Bridle

A day or two after the first saddling, I introduce the young horse to wearing a bit. The saddling should be easy by now, so it's an appropriate time to add something new. I use a D-ring or O-ring smooth snaffle bit, and a bridle without reins. The horse will be wearing his halter and a longe line, so I just slip the bridle on over the halter. The bridle should fit properly, with the snaffle bit pulled

When introducing the bridle, I slip it over the horse's halter.

up into his mouth high enough so that one or two wrinkles are visible on both sides of his lips. If the bit is too low the horse can get his tongue over it, which is very uncomfortable.

I leave the bridle on for the entire session. If the horse is really dissatisfied with the bitting process, I tie him to the wall with the halter and lead rope for a while, but leave the reinless bridle on over the halter so he can spend time getting used to it by chewing on and playing with it. I stay out of the picture, so he educates himself.

If he is still chewing and fighting the reinless bridle a couple of sessions later, I let him eat while he wears it, making sure he is in a safe stall where the bit can't be hooked on anything. I check on him frequently.

This entire bitting process should only take a day or two at the most. If it takes longer, contact an equine dentist for a check-up. A horse may possibly have retained caps, wolf teeth, or sharp enamel points, which are interfering with the comfort of the bit.

I adjust the bridle so that the snaffle is high enough to produce one or two wrinkles on both sides of his lips. A horse can get his tongue over a bit that hangs too low.

If the colt shows dissatisfaction with the bit, I will tie him to the wall with the halter rope (he wears a reinless bridle).

I don't proceed to the next steps—"tying around" and ground driving—until the horse is no longer trying to rid his mouth of the bit. He must show me that he's comfortable in the bridle.

Tying Around

Tying the horse's head around teaches a horse to follow his nose and "give," or submit to the bridle. After the normal longe time and saddling ritual, I put split reins on the snaffle bridle. I'll tie the horse's head around with the inside rein attached to the rear cinch billet D-ring and the much looser outside rein attached to the saddle horn, just enough to tip his nose so that he has to bend and thus walk in a tight circle in the round pen. I don't tie him so short and tight that he can't get some slack when he responds. To excessively tighten the inside rein would cause discomfort and not offer enough slack once the horse yields to the pressure and begins moving around in a circle.

When I first tie a horse around, I walk in a tight circle with him. He'll follow me, turning his front end toward me, and his hip to the

I tie the horse's head around to tip his nose.

Close-up of how it is tied to the saddle.

How to run the rein in order to tie it.

I won't tie a horse so short that he can't create some slack when he responds by giving to the pressure.

outside of the circle. I then stroll outside the circle, leaving him to work on his own. After he is tied in one direction for ten minutes, I tie him around to the other and leave him for another ten minutes.

It's important to keep a close watch on a horse that's tied around. Sometimes, he'll fool you. He may seem to be a quick study for the first five minutes, doing everything perfectly. You give yourself a big pat on the back, but what you don't realize is that there's likely to be a wreck by minute six or seven.

He might grow tired of the game and begin to resist or fight the bridle. If it's not a frantic situation—if he's not fighting so hard that he might fall down or otherwise hurt himself, I just observe his actions and allow him to experiment and fight himself without intervention. By staying out of it, I make sure that he will learn more and won't associate anyone with the mess he has created for himself.

But if he falls or gets hung up in the fence or equipment, you have to get in quickly and offer assistance by untying the rein. This is why it's important to stay close. When I tie a young horse around, I either stand outside the round pen but close by, or I ride an older horse around him, or near enough so I can keep a constant watch on the youngster.

If the young horse is staying calm but not yielding to the bridle, I do one of two things. I use a bungee cord tied to the back of the saddle with the inside rein (the left rein if he's turning to the left) tied to it. This works for a horse that is really fighting and not wanting to yield. He learns from the cord's flexibility that there is an immediate reward when he yields to the pressure. If he resists, the pull is not unyielding, but just a soft tug. The other option is to ride another horse past him. That will trick him into moving because he will want to turn to look. Soon he figures out the puzzle and begins to yield.

Some horses give to rein pressure easily right from the start. For example, horses with a lot of Thoroughbred blood seem to be softer in the mouth than the more cold-blooded types. As a general rule, a horse that is "shallow mouthed" will be softer and more responsive to the bit than a horse that has a deeper mouth. I classify a horse as shallow mouthed if he measures about four inches or less from the top, where the bit sets and pulls up on the lips, to the bottom where the teeth meet. Softer-mouthed horses begin giving to the pressure quickly. They might have some resistance and fight at first, but they generally figure it out pretty fast.

Ground Driving

Ground driving is a beneficial way to teach a horse to guide and steer with direct rein pressure before beginning to ride. This step is extra insurance that offers greater control over the horse once you climb aboard. The horse will become accustomed to hearing instruction come from behind him rather than from the front, which up to this point is where the handler has been. Ground driving also is one more place to get the horse accustomed to potential distractions that can occur. Allowing the driving lines to swing and touch all up and down the horse's hind legs, under his tail area, and over his croup further "sacks out," or desensitizes, the horse.

The first time I drive a young horse will be in the round pen. I saddle, longe, and bridle him, then tie the stirrups under his belly. When I longe, I usually let the stirrups flop all over to get the horse used to being touched in that area. But when I drive a horse, I want the stirrups still and secure because I run my driving lines through them. Stirrups that aren't tied under the belly allow too much swing in the lines and therefore tangle the lines so it's hard to control the horse's forward motion. It becomes too easy for a horse to wheel around and face me. If he does and the stirrups are not secured, it's difficult to move him back to the position where he needs to be.

I attach a long pair of driving lines to the snaffle bit and run them through the stirrups to my hands. The reins *must* be long enough so I'm out of the way of the back feet, should the horse kick. Eight to ten feet of line behind the horse is a good safety measure.

First I swing the lines a bit to get the horse used to the feel. Then I pull on my left rein and, at the same time, touch him with the looser right rein on his hip to encourage him to go forward. If he jumps forward, I give him some slack. He shouldn't be disciplined for this movement. As long as he's in the round pen, there is still control without pulling or hanging on him, both of which will deaden the feel of his mouth.

The more the horse feels the lines all over, the more he desensitizes, which is what I'm after. I swing the lines all over him, including up and down his hind legs. From the standpoint of future safety, this is a good investment in time. What if something touched the horse's fetlocks some day, and he wasn't desensitized in that area? Somebody could be kicked. What if someday, you are leading or ponying another horse and the lead rope ended up under the horse's tail? If that area were desensitized through ground driving, the reaction would be minimal. Without it, the outcome could be devastating.

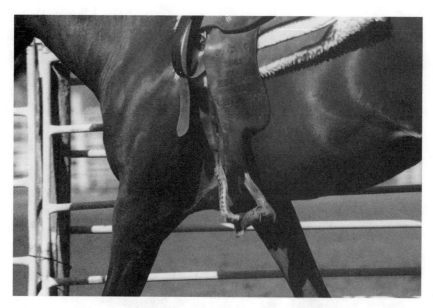

When I first longe the horse under saddle, I let the stirrups swing loose so that he becomes used to them bumping against his sides.

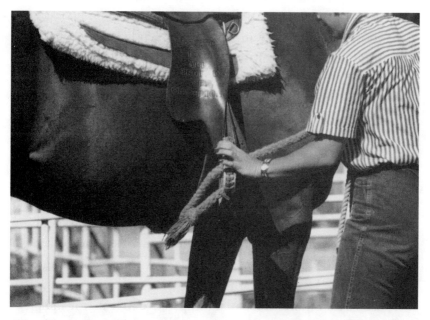

When I ground drive a horse, I tie the stirrups with a rope under his belly so that they stay still and do not cause the driving lines to tangle.

I touch the horse all over with the driving lines, including up and down his hind legs.

To move the horse forward, I slap him gently on the rump with the outside line. Let's say I want to move him off to the right. The right line will come from the stirrup to my hand in a straight line. The left line will be below his buttocks and above his hock. I stand on his right in the "drive" position of his flight zone. He basically travels around me as though he's being longed, but he's between two lines.

The worst thing that can happen is that the horse wheels around to face me. I want to keep him moving forward away from me, bending around and learning how to give to the bit. The horse was used to taking orders from me when I was in front of him. Now, he needs to do the same while I am behind him. When we worked on the follow-the-leader system, the horse was learning through his language. Now, he has to learn mine.

There's a transition here, and it's imperative to realize it and practice patience as the horse becomes used to a handler moving from a longe position to one directly behind him. Typically, he will want to

The ground driving movement is initially similar to longeing. I remain in the center of the round pen and work the colt in a circle around me.

turn and face the person. Pulling on his face isn't an option here, so I just step back and slap him on the hind end with the line once more to move him forward. If he becomes scared because I'm behind him, he might try to bolt instead of turning to face me. In that case, I pull his face toward the middle of the round pen, begin a longe circle, and keep him in it until he quiets down. Then I work my way back to a position behind him, where I can drive him at a walk.

When I start asking a horse to turn, I use my fingers on the inside rein to encourage him to give to the bridle and move around. If he needs more pressure to convince him to turn, I add a little pull, but then instantly release the pressure when he yields, even if it's just one step. Then, I keep him moving around the round pen.

Stopping and Backing with Driving Lines

After the horse has learned to walk ahead of me and turn in both directions, I can teach him to stop by saying "whoa." The word

I then step back and drive him from behind.

should be very familiar to him by this time, because of the previous voice work. But if he has a memory lapse, I pull on both reins at the same time I again say "whoa." It's not a tug-o-war and not a jerk. A solid pull should only be used if he seems to be having a memory lapse about what "whoa" means. If a solid pull is necessary, keep your feet in front of you and balance yourself so you won't be pulled forward into his hindquarters.

I release the pressure as soon as he stops and let the horse stand there for a minute or two until I know he's calm and comfortable and isn't anticipating any maneuvers. Then I teach him how to back.

I add some rein pressure with a seesaw, give-and-take motion using alternating hands. If the horse takes even one step back, I slacken the lines as a reward and walk up to his side near his hindquarters and give him a pat. I then encourage him to move forward, bend in each direction, and again stop and back. Maybe the next time he'll give me two steps. He just has to show me that he has the idea and that he's willing to try.

All Aboard

The first time I climb aboard a young horse in the round pen, the horse will be wearing a snaffle bridle with his halter over it and a longe line attached to the halter. A handler on the ground holds the longe line as I mount. I turn the horse's head toward me for control in case he decides to lunge or buck. If he does so, I am set up to pull him into a tight circle and step down to get off of him. Stepping off, if it becomes necessary, prevents me from getting bucked off, as well as allowing me to stay in control of the situation.

Once I'm in the saddle and know I can stay there, I do no more than sit on the young horse for a few minutes, allowing him a little time to take in the sensation of having someone astride him. Then I ask the handler to lead the horse around in a tight circle. The handler stands toward the middle of the round pen, more or less pulling the horse around. Gradually this movement begins to look like a longe circle, and the work area can become increasingly larger as the young horse becomes more confident.

If the horse does decide to jump, I pull his head around toward the center, stop his forward motion, and allow him a few moments to settle before we return to a relaxed walk. I avoid overreacting at all costs.

Once the young horse is moving around quietly, I ask the handler to unsnap the longe line and leave the round pen. I don't remove this safety line until I am secure with the young mount. This might happen on the first ride, but with some horses it might take until the fourth or fifth time I've been in the saddle. The secret here is to keep things positive with no bad experiences.

Before I consider taking the horse into the big arena, I spend time in the round pen establishing that he and I can walk, trot, canter, stop, back, and turn in each direction. And, of course, I want him well-schooled to the voice command "whoa." It might take from two rides to six rides, depending on the horse's learning pace. Some horses are very accepting and eager to learn, while others are more timid and require more time and patience.

Avoid Too Much Round Pen Work

Be careful, though, about spending too much time in the round pen. Soundness problems can result from too much work in tight circles. Tendon soreness can occur, as well as other types of soreness. However, splints are probably the biggest concern with working in too small a circle. They cause an ugly blemish, as well as possible lameness, and layoff time will result if the horse fractures his splint bone.

I don't want a young horse in the round pen for any more rides than necessary. Once the spook factor is under control, I take him out of the round pen and into the big arena. If he needs more time, I keep him in the round pen a few days more, but I don't think I've ever ridden a horse in the round pen more than five or six days before attempting the big arena.

Not only are soundness issues at stake, but training problems can result from too much round pen work. Subsequent chapters will show that a big part of my program revolves around getting a horse to lift his shoulders and use them properly. At this round pen stage, he hasn't yet learned much about this movement. But, future learning can be sabotaged if early on he develops the habit of dropping his inside shoulder.

In the next chapters, you will learn about the first few months under saddle, about the calisthenic exercises, and starting transitions and finish work. I'll give general guidelines on when certain tasks can be introduced. But always keep in mind that horses handle training based on different mental and physical levels and strength. While one horse might be ready quickly, another might need more time. Patience is indeed a virtue here.

7

THE FIRST FEW MONTHS UNDER SADDLE

Out of the round corral, into the arena

————————◄o►————————

B efore I tell you what I do with my horses during the first few months under saddle, I'll tell you what I do not do: I do not work on headsets.

Too many people concentrate on trying to make a horse set his head in the beginning of their training programs. Instead, they should strive for control of the shoulders and hips. The headset will come later, as the horse becomes stronger and learns how to propel his body through self-carriage.

A horse's headset should be the result of proper body movement accomplished by driving from behind with his haunches, rounding his back, and lifting his shoulders. If his body works correctly, his head and neck are easier to place in the desired position. But it will be a few months before he is ready to work on head and neck carriage. When it happens, he will begin to surf, or stretch, his head and neck out in front of him, discovering that this level topline position gives him balance. A natural, level topline will result, which is an imaginary line that starts at the horse's poll or the tip of his ears, extends down the top of his neck, across the top of his back and croup. The topline should not be forced or gained through artificial means, such as early use of headset gimmicks.

There is also a strength issue to consider. Especially in the first thirty days of riding, a young horse doesn't have the strength to keep his head and neck consistently in a "show pen headset" without traveling "downhill"—too heavy on his forehand. At this stage attempts at teaching the mechanics of lifting his shoulders would be in vain. During the first few months under saddle, as a young horse learns to lift his shoulders and balance himself, he might need to travel with his head higher than what is considered desirable in the show arena. If it helps me to control his shoulders and keep them lifted, I allow a young horse to go at least three to four months before I ask for the start of a consistent headset. Then, I teach him to drop at the withers and start to find a frame with his shoulders up and his neck out in front of him, balanced and relaxed. (Chapter 9 will explain how I accomplish this position.)

During this "pre-headset" time, a horse must still give to the bit when the rider applies pressure on the reins. He must not resist by rooting against the bridle or tossing his head. For example, if the rider applies a direct rein to the right, the horse should move his nose to the right, slightly lowering his head and neck before the rider releases the pressure. When the horse gives properly to the pressure, he should be rewarded by the rider's release of hand pressure.

During the "pre-headset" work in this chapter, it will be up to you to decide how much time is needed on simpler tasks like walking circles, or how fast you move your horse into serpentines, crossovers, and other exercises. Remember—we're talking months, not days. As you become attuned to your horse, he'll tell you through his actions when it's time to try something more difficult. If he accepts a new task with ease, he will appear relaxed. Wringing his tail, pinning his ears, or resisting leg pressure by moving toward the pressure instead of away from it are all signs that he is having trouble with the new task. Revert to something easy that he has done before, like walking and trotting circles. Then after a day or two, challenge him again with new information.

Give your young horse a few months to become coordinated. Big, highly bred horses with a lot of Thoroughbred breeding experience a great deal of growth as two- and three-year-olds. They're gangly, with long necks and thin legs, none of which seem to travel easily in the same direction. To pressure this type of horse to become coordinated is akin to asking a six-foot-tall, thirteen-year-old girl to be a perfect basketball player. No matter how harsh the demands, she will be incapable at that age of doing her best. Her legs will hurt, and she will want to quit. It's better to let her mature slowly and grow into herself, keeping the game fun and doable. In a few years she will have the strength and body control to accept the high-pressure demands of excelling in college or on the pro court.

Similarly, give your horse time to develop. This is not an overnight process. You'll be thrilled with the results if you allow your horse to progress at the pace best for him. If the young horse is pressured to establish this coordination too quickly, you'll be the one doing all the work to support the horse with excess hand and leg aids. Your goal of producing a horse with the coveted self-carriage will go right down the drain.

It all starts with that first ride in the big arena.

Getting Down to Business

Going from the round pen into the big arena is an important day in the learning process of a young horse. Some accept the day with grace, others with jitters.

If the horse is quiet, I walk him in some slow circles, about forty feet in diameter. If he stays relaxed, I move him into a sitting trot and continue circling. Most will relax promptly and easily in this new environment. But if one acts scared of having a rider on his back and tries to race off, I use direct-rein pressure to slow him down into a tighter circle and make him walk.

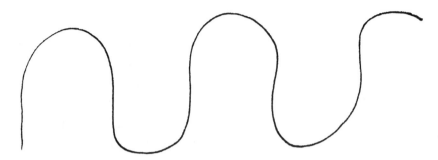

Serpentines are a series of U-turns.

Once the horse is giving to the direct-rein pressure and follow-ing his nose with his shoulders, therefore guiding well, I will begin working him in serpentines. The best way to describe serpentines is to equate them to a series of consecutive half circles or U-turns performed in alternating directions. When I serpentine a horse, I use direct- and indirect-rein and leg pressure as I did with circles. Not only do these connected "U's" control his speed and rhythm; it keeps him busy, gets his mind off being frightened, and instills confidence. He takes on an "I can do this" frame of mind, because I show him that he can, indeed, perform this task.

I incorporate circles and serpentines into the routine with all my horses, and for a good reason. In the beginning circles are used primarily for teaching the young horse to pack the rider's weight.

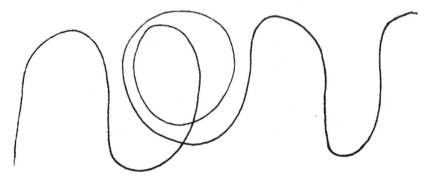

A mix of serpentines and circles keeps the horse waiting for my cues rather than anticipating and working on his own.

As he masters weight-carrying, circles teach him to work lightly off the aids—following his nose from rein pressure, and moving away from my outside leg and around my inside leg helps the horse establish a nice arch with his body.

Proper use of direct-rein and leg pressure helps the horse understand what to do. For example, if I want to bring the horse into a circle to the right, my right, or direct, rein guides the horse by pulling his nose into the direction I want him to travel. Hence, he is learning to follow his nose and yield to the pressure of the bit. I use pressure with my left leg to encourage him to move forward and maintain the arc of the circle. My right (inside) leg stabilizes his inside shoulder and keeps it from dropping to the inside of the circle. If you want to get control of the shoulders, you have to get the horse light and responsive in the bridle and to leg aids.

To encourage lateral movement of the horse's head and neck, when tracking to the right, I keep my right (direct-rein) hand low and out to the side about twelve inches from the pommel of the saddle. The first time or two that I ride a young horse in circles or serpentines I rely on direct rein only, but as the horse begins giving to the pressure readily and has a clear understanding of "following his nose," I add indirect-rein pressure. This is possible after two to six rides during which I have ridden the horse in "beginner" circles and serpentines. Now, he will be ready to accept the additional cue of the indirect rein.

When I ride in a circle to the right, I hold the indirect (left) rein higher than the right (direct rein), at about four inches above the pommel. It rests on the left side of the horse's neck. Teamed with the pressure I apply with my left leg, a barrier is created that keeps the horse moving in an arc to the right. His left shoulder is blocked, so he can't drift to the left when he should be traveling right. He gets the message that his shoulders must follow his nose.

As the horse's skill level increases, I keep my hands closer together because the cues can be more subtle. Using the direct rein supported with the indirect rein helps me contain and control the horse's shoulder region even more, a primer for later work on isolating and moving the shoulders.

I continue to advance the horse through the training process by combining serpentines and circles. To serpentine to the right, I apply pressure with the right (direct) rein to bend the horse's nose into the direction of the turn. I use the left (indirect) rein lightly on his neck. Then I add just enough pressure with my left calf against the horse's side to encourage him to move forward and maintain the arc. My right leg lies softly against the horse's right side to support his shoulders. Be careful not to apply so much pressure with the inside (right) leg that the horse feels there is no open place to move.

To change directions to make a left serpentine, just reverse the aids. A left turn becomes left direct rein, right indirect rein, right leg pressure to maintain arc, and left leg pressure to support the horse's shoulders.

Serpentines incorporate straight-line work before and after each U-turn. I vary the number of steps. If the horse maintains his speed and cadence, such as a medium sitting trot with regular rhythm, I trot him for about ten to twenty steps before applying the aids to ask for a U-turn. However, if he is inconsistent in his speed and cadence, I trot him only four or five steps before asking for the turn. The serpentines encourage him to slow down if he is moving too quickly and to pace himself if he is out of cadence. Incorporating a series of circles at this time will also help reestablish pace and cadence before returning to the serpentine work.

When he is on the straight line in between each turn, I release the rein and leg pressure. I begin to add the rein and leg aids about three steps before the turn to get him set up, rather than just snatching at the rein the instant I want the turn.

Mixing serpentines and circles keeps the horse attentive and waiting for your cues, rather than anticipating the next move. A horse that is worked in a set pattern such as left-right-left serpentines over and over again sets himself up to do it on his own. He will often dive into a turn before his rider asks, which is a bad habit that needs to be headed off. I mix circles and serpentines all over the arena with no real pattern or number of times. I also vary the size of the circles. Even though I'm in the big arena, I ride in about a forty-foot radius at first. I circle one direction, then the other, then close the circle down to a twenty-foot range. Then I make it larger. Everything is random. Large, small, left, right—the horse never knows which direction he should travel in, until I ask. This sense of surprise teaches him to wait for the cues, which is a strongly desirable trait in any training program.

Using Your Legs

During serpentines, the young horse definitely feels my leg aids. There is no reason for a rider to be afraid of moving his or her legs when riding a young horse. I let my legs bump gently against the horse's sides while he moves to desensitize him to the feel. I don't want him to become dead-sided, but I do want him to feel leg pressure, such as when I ask for that serpentine turn. However, I never want him to panic when he feels my legs move. Some horses go ballistic if you slap their sides with a stirrup fender, spooking away in fear. You don't want that with any horse, especially one you'll eventually ride with a lot of lower leg pressure in a hunt saddle. The horse must stay with the rider's legs and not scurry forward once leg pressure is applied. In addition to determining direction of movement and offering support of the horse's body parts, leg aids should ask for forward motion without being a signal for the horse to blindly speed ahead.

If a horse becomes frantic when my legs bump him, I put him into a set of tight serpentines to maintain control. I continue to bounce my legs against his sides until he relaxes. I want a horse to accept the help I give him with my leg aids. These serpentines can be done at both the walk and sitting trot. The sitting trot helps to keep the horse's legs slow as he learns to respond to my hand and leg aids. Working on lengthening the horse's stride at the trot will come later in the training progression.

No Spurs Yet

I don't use spurs on a young horse for the first two weeks that I ride him. I spend that spurless time getting him used to my legs banging around on his sides. It also gives me time to gauge the horse's response to leg aids.

Some horses are so responsive to leg aids that I'll never have to ride them with spurs. But if a young horse is lazy about moving off my leg or is just not sensitive on his sides, I begin to use spurs as an extension of my leg aids. If I "ask" for a response by squeezing his side with my calf and he doesn't move away from the pressure, I "tell" him with light spur pressure. There is never any jabbing or punishing.

I use ball spurs on young horses. Rather than rowel or otherwise sharp points, ball spurs are just what the name implies—round, ball-shaped ends. As with any spur, they are to be used solely as aids and not as weapons.

When It's Time to Canter

Before I ask for a canter, I want to be sure my horse knows the meaning of "whoa" and I know that I can keep him in a circle for control. I keep him in a sixty-foot circle, rather than cantering him along the rail. This is larger than the twenty- to forty-foot circles I used for initial walk and sitting trot. A young horse will probably be uncoordinated in his first attempts at cantering with a rider, and he'll need a larger circle in which to work.

I start by circling in a sitting trot, guiding him with direct-rein pressure. I support his outside shoulder with some pressure on the indirect rein, and support his rib cage with my outside leg at the girth. For example, to travel to the right, I apply pressure on the right (direct) rein, and a little less pressure to the left (indirect or "outside") rein. I apply pressure with my left (outside) leg, then I make a "kiss" noise. The horse will recognize this voice command from his groundwork but may be reluctant to canter off. Therefore, I will bump his sides with both my legs working together at the girth until he moves off into the canter. On these first few canter attempts, I will take this gait any way I can get it. This might include using the ends of my reins to slap the horse lightly on the rump. Eventually he will remember that the voice command (kissing) was used in his round pen work to encourage him to canter.

During these attempts to get the horse to canter, a rider's hands must be soft and not hang on the bridle. In fact, when the horse starts to move ahead and is clearly going into the canter, rein pressure should be released. If the rider doesn't free the horse's head at this point, the bridle is telling him "stop," while the rider's legs are attempting to kick him into a canter. That clashing of cues is like driving a car with one foot on the brake and the other on the accelerator. The horse needs clear cues.

Keep in mind that the first canter could be fast and clumsy. Typically young horses will canter only a few strides at first, then break down into a trot. Each subsequent time the horse is asked for the canter, he will be more comfortable with the process, become more balanced, and increase the amount of time he will maintain the gait.

Let's Talk Leads

Don't expect a young horse to be perfectly balanced the first time you ask for the canter. There is a chance he won't get everything right, and will take the wrong lead. A lead is determined by how far in front of the outside legs the inside hind and front legs are traveling. For example, if the horse is cantering in a circle to the right on his right lead, his inside right front and hind legs will move further forward than his outside left legs. He is able to maintain his balance even in a tight circle because the inside legs are supporting him.

It is possible for a horse to travel on the correct lead with his front leg, but be on the wrong lead behind. Called crossfiring or cross-cantering, it is undesirable because of the lack of balance it creates.

Watching a horse move at a canter in the round pen will give me a clue as to how easy—or hard—it is for him to travel on the correct lead. Like left-handed or right-handed people, some horses favor one lead over another, and the tendency to travel this way will show up consistently. What did he show you in the round pen? Did he always take the correct lead with both his front and back legs? That means it's easy for him. But, if he took the wrong lead or crossfired each time he cantered, it's going to take work and patience from the saddle to teach him which lead he must travel on.

When starting to canter in the big arena, the horse might take the incorrect lead. His gait will feel very uncoordinated. He will need to be interrupted. Simply use the reins to bring him back into a trot, and then restart the canter. Repeat this step until he begins traveling on the correct lead. Pay attention to how he is balancing himself. If his head is overflexed to the inside of the circle with your direct rein, his hip will swing to the outside of the circle and onto the incorrect lead. Try using less direct-rein pressure so that he still understands he's to travel in a circle, but his body will be straight enough that he can balance his weight on his outside legs. This way, he will be able to lift his inside shoulder and strike out on the inside (correct) lead.

It might take a few days before a horse that is, for example, extremely left-leaded, to become comfortable traveling on the right lead.

Assessing Talent

Once the horse is moving at the canter and on the correct lead, I study his movement to assess his natural talent. While he canters through three revolutions of a sixty-foot circle, I pay attention to whether he is speeding up or slowing down. If a horse gradually slows, I know that this is a horse that wants to go slow. It will be easy to get this horse to the point where he eventually stays slow and consistent.

The opposite is true with the horse that starts off cantering slow and gains speed. I know that this horse is more comfortable at a faster gait and that I'll need to do a lot of work to teach him that "slow is the way to go."

I'm not consumed with this assessment. I just do it early so I'll be aware of what's ahead. With a horse that moves out fast for five or six strides and then wants to slow down, I'll let him canter and find his natural speed and stay there for a while. If he canters three or four circles, he'll find his natural rhythm. The more natural rhythm, pace, and cadence the horse has, the easier your job will be.

With a horse that starts cantering slow and wants to speed up, I'm careful not to canter him very long. I stop him while he's still cantering slowly. The minute I feel his weight shift forward to speed up, I ask him to stop and back up. This type of horse will start calisthenics work much sooner than the naturally slow horse, in order to teach him to use his hindquarters and pace his canter cadence.

I wait longer to start calisthenics with the horse that wants to canter leisurely in his circles, because he has more natural balance and cadence. So, he should have a little more opportunity to develop these skills on his own before a rider intervenes with advanced calisthenics. I'll confine the cantering to working in circles for at least ninety days before I begin the basic canter calisthenics.

Stopping From the Canter

To stop a horse from the canter, I give the voice command, "whoa," then sit back and relax my seat down into the saddle. I want the horse to collect himself and stop on his own without having to pull on his mouth. This is the first step of the horse's introduction to self-carriage. The horse that learns to collect and stop on his haunches on his own has mastered "self-carriage, step one."

This is a trainer-specific technique. There are certainly hunter under saddle horses that are spur broke, which means the rider squeezes with their legs for the horse to stop. This isn't a technique that I use, because most of my horses go on to show in pattern equitation classes. I find that it's easier for youth and amateur riders to ride a pattern on a horse that is not spur broke, because for most people it is more logical for them to use their leg aids to get the horse to move forward or speed up rather than stop. Therefore, in the pressure of competition, less subconscious communication errors are made from a nervous rider when riding a pattern horse that is not spur broke.

With my verbal command and intentional lack of rein pressure, my hunter under saddle horses often come to a halt looking rather like reiners doing a sliding stop. This isn't what we ultimately want in a hunter under saddle horse, but it is the building block for downward transitions (to be addressed in the next chapter). The crisp, well-balanced stop indicates that the horse is using his haunches and that his weight is balanced back onto his hindquarters, both are extremely desirable. In an ideal stop from the canter, the horse initiates the stop from his haunches rather than from the forehand. The weight must be shifted back. If not, it creates too much weight on the forehand.

The only time my hands will take an active role in the stop is when a horse doesn't obey my "stop" request. I pull him down with the reins, then back him up. The pull-down and back-up work disciplines him, so he learns that he is to stop immediately from the word "whoa," with his weight on his haunches. Use of the "ask, tell, demand" technique is a definite must here.

Body Basics

Three maneuvers that will also help a horse to learn to use his body can be taught during the first few months under saddle. All are excellent foundation exercises for the horse to have mastered by the time he begins calisthenics, transition, and finishing work. These moves are the sidepass, the turn on the haunches, and the turn on the forehand. These exercises should be practiced in both the left and right directions. For clarity in explanation, I will concentrate on the cues to the right, which can be easily reversed to perform the same maneuvers to the left.

Teaching the Sidepass

It is important to have control over the horse's shoulders and hips to teach a horse to sidepass. For a sidepass to the right, tighten your left rein, which will bend the horse's head and neck slightly to the left. Use your left calf at the girth to apply leg pressure.

Use your right rein to stabilize the shoulders, keeping them straight and preventing them from over-rotating to the right.

Allow your horse to move to the right by making sure he has an "opening" created by lack of leg aids on the right side. In the beginning, it will work best to move the shoulders a step to the right, then use leg pressure (left leg for a move to the right) to move the hips to the right and "catch up" with the shoulders. During these moves, the left front and left hind legs should cross over and in front of the right ones.

Using a fence to teach a horse to sidepass prevents him from moving forward, away from your leg pressure. Facing the fence blocks his forward motion so that he better understands that he is to move to the side.

When he has mastered the basics, take him away from the fence and venture out to the middle of the arena. By now you should be able to sidepass him with his body straight, moving his shoulders and hips in unison without the counter arc (bend to the left) that was used in the first few lessons.

Turn on the Forehand

These are the steps in teaching a turn on the forehand, again using a turn to the right as an example. (1) Establish contact with the right rein. (2) Move your right leg back slightly behind the girth and apply pressure to the horse's rib cage to move his haunches clockwise. (3) Use your left rein to block the left shoulder and keep

To sidepass to the right, move the horse's head and neck slightly to the left and apply pressure with your left leg.

The right rein stabilizes the shoulders and keeps them straight.

Then move the horse's hips with pressure from your left leg so that they "catch up" with the shoulders.

Using a fence when teaching a horse to sidepass will prevent him from moving forward rather than laterally.

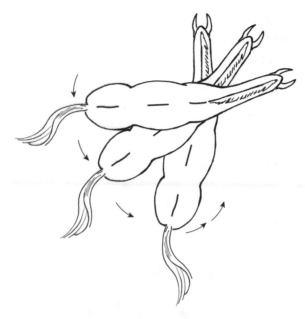

The turn on the forehand: the horse's front feet must stay put as the pivot point while the hind feet rotate around them.

As the horse becomes coordinated, his right foot becomes the pivot point for the right turn on the forehand.

it from moving to the left in a sidepass motion. His front end should remain in one place while the hind end "travels" in a circle around his front end. As he becomes more coordinated, his right front foot will be the pivot point.

Turn on the Haunches

To execute a turn on the haunches to the right: (1) Move both reins to the right until your indirect rein crosses over the horse's mane. Match your hands as though you were holding a twelve-inch rod between them. (2) Add pressure with your left leg directly behind the girth, to move the shoulders around the haunches in a clockwise direction. The horse should pivot around his right hind foot.

As you work your horse during these first few months, vary his routine so that you don't work on a particular move for a long time. This variety will keep him more receptive to learning.

With any of these moves, reward the horse for trying, even if he takes just one or two steps when you ask him to sidepass, or do a turn on the forehand or haunches. Release your aids, and pat him

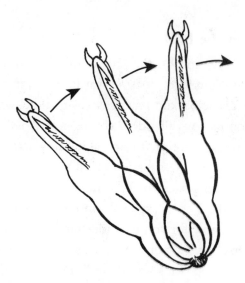

The turn on the haunches: The hind feet remain stationary as the front feet rotate around them.

Move both reins to the right, keeping your hands level as though you were holding a twelve-inch rod between them.

on the neck. In subsequent lessons, you can gradually ask for more steps.

Don't Ride on the Rail

During the first few months, the only thing done on the rail—with the exception of using it to block forward motion in the beginning sidepass work—is the backup practice explained below. For the first four to five months I won't ride a young horse forward along the rail. After that time, however, I start taking him around the rail for brief periods of time, often just a partial revolution of the arena. Then I take him right back to the center of the arena to work on more fundamentals. This is explained in more detail in Chapter 9, but it's important now for you to understand why you should keep your young horse off the rail at this stage. He shouldn't associate the rail as "the road to somewhere." He should never think, "Hey—if I get down to the end of this rail, I get to go around the corner. Then, I'm at the gate. And that's a good place because it's close to the barn."

Rather than thinking about getting to a certain place, he needs to focus on moving his body and staying in a frame.

The Last Move of Every Ride

The last thing I do with every ride is to practice backing the horse. Because all my other maneuvers are done in the center of the arena, the practice back is the only thing I consistently do on the rail, starting with the first ride.

I walk the horse on the rail. With the verbal "whoa," command, I ask him to stop on a loose rein. Then I pick up my reins and ask him to back. The number of steps I demand depends on how familiar the horse is with backing. I want him to give to the pressure of the bridle and not resist by rooting his head up into the air. When he yields properly to rein pressure and takes a step back, I immediately reward him with the release of rein pressure.

I want him to look forward to this backing practice and view it as a reward at the end of his ride. Using the back as a reward for a finished ride is important because some ride time is spent using the backup as a way to correct a poor stop. And soon you'll use it as a way to correct for a poor canter departure or a racy canter cadence. The young horse shouldn't associate every backup with discipline, because backing is a required element of each hunter under saddle class and must be done without fear or resistance. Therefore, putting a show backup practice at the end of every ride helps the horse associate a nice, soft backup with the end of his training session, and not just as a correction for a poor maneuver.

This backup practice on the rail needs to be relaxed so that the horse can tell it's not discipline. He needs to clearly see it as a reward. After I back him, I stand him quietly on the rail before I dismount and loosen the cinch. Dismounting, there at the rail, emphasizes the reward. It also keeps the horse honest later at a show; he'll want to stay on the rail instead of cutting into the center of the arena or stopping at the gate.

Look How Much You've Accomplished!

When your horse has learned all of the skills and maneuvers described in this chapter and is ready to graduate to calisthenics and transitions and then onto finishing work, take time to reflect on the wonderful job you've both done. You can see now why I emphasized in the beginning that training the hunter under saddle horse is a "process" that takes a long time. But taking the time to cultivate the learning in such a lasting way is certainly worth the effort.

WHAT IF HE SPOOKS?

There are often surprises when riding young horses, and one of those big surprises happens when the horse spooks. It will usually be in one of two ways. The first is the more radical. He will bolt to get away from something, such as a cow on the outside of the arena. The arena fence will eventually stop him. To allow the horse to run into a fence in an attempt to stop him causes a wreck. Instead, I wait until the horse is near the fence, then say "whoa" and apply give-and-take pressure on the reins to take his attention away from whatever it was that scared him. This action slows him down and makes it easier to turn him into a tight circle to gain control. The most important thing in this situation is that the horse sees the fence when he gets close to it and does not injure himself or his rider by slamming into or going over the fence.

The second type of spooking is not as drastic. A horse will be moving cooperatively in a big circle, but is afraid of an object, such as a garbage can, that he sees on the other side of the arena fence. He tries to avoid it by cutting in ten feet toward the center of his circle. I won't get upset, but simply continue his circles and do not react when he passes the garbage can and moves away from it. I ignore the problem and soon he is traveling in a correct circle and past the garbage can without incident.

To stop and heavily discipline the horse for this type of spooking increases his fear and makes him even more inclined to spook in the future. The situation is best handled by continuing forward, without reaction from the rider. It convinces the horse that it was silly to be afraid. After all, his rider didn't worry about that garbage can, so why should he?

Another method of instilling confidence is to ride the horse to the garbage can at the end of the session. Walk him on the rail by the can, stop and do the "last move of the ride," the practice back. This way, the horse is rewarded at the end of the ride for staying quiet and calm beside the very object that previously worried him.

I've ridden so many young horses that I'm at ease in these situations. If you're not, and your young horse is spooky in the big arena, I strongly suggest you get an experienced helper to ride a quiet "pony" horse and lead your horse around with you in the saddle. This requires putting a halter and long rope on your horse along with the snaffle bridle. The key is to make sure your horse was ponied before you started to ride him so he's at ease with the situation. He'll gain confidence from the older horse and will soon be ready to be ridden solo.

IF YOU WANT TO "GO ENGLISH" IN THE FIRST FEW MONTHS

Exactly when you change from a western to a hunt-seat saddle will be a matter of choice influenced by your own riding ability and your horse's training progress. I can't make that decision for you, but I can give you some cautions and guidelines.

The hunt saddle is more of a close-contact style than a western saddle. There are less "leather parts," especially when comparing western fenders to English stirrup leathers. When you switch to a hunt saddle, your horse feels your legs more as you lay them against his sides. If you've let your legs gently bounce against him and have used your legs in teaching serpentines, the sidepass, and turns on the forehand and haunches, the added leg pressure from the hunt saddle should not be an issue. However, some horses are more touchy than others. It's not so much the new feel against their sides, but the pressure points on the back. (See the chapter on tack.) That's why correct saddle fit is extremely important.

One young stallion I rode was so irritated by having a well-fitted hunt saddle on his back that he showed his displeasure by bucking. He didn't like the difference in fit and feel. I had to spend extra time riding him in a hunt saddle to get him to accept it.

I'm in no hurry to change my horses over to the hunt saddle, but I won't wait until the day of the first show before I find out if the horse will accept the change. Two weeks to a month before the first show, I will ride a young horse in a hunt saddle for the first time just to be sure of how they accept it. Most horses will be fine and offer no adverse reactions. I like using the western saddle for schooling, so I return to using the western saddle until a few days before the show, then I ride in the hunt saddle continually through show day.

Your balance and leg strength should also be deciding factors. If you are unsteady in your seat and don't have a steady lower leg a young horse might unseat you if he spooks or otherwise makes a quick move. This could cause an additional disaster if you wear spurs when you ride, because you might hook the horse in the flank or another sensitive area when you are off balance.

It's important that you are able to use your hands, seat, and legs independently. Specifically, you shouldn't use the reins to brace against for balance, or drive your feet forward

Practice posting in the western saddle before riding your young horse in a hunt saddle.

and sit on your "back pockets" in an attempt to find a balance point. Posting should be coordinated and controlled.

If you need work on your basic hunt-seat skills and are lacking in strength, you will benefit from practicing on an older trained horse that isn't likely to be bothered by unbalanced movement.

Once you have fine-tuned your skills, I suggest that you spend some time posting in the western saddle to get your young horse used to the movement, before you switch to the hunt saddle. Remember that if you try the hunt saddle and things don't work out at first, you can always switch back to schooling in the western saddle, even when schooling at a show.

{ 8 }

CALISTHENICS AND TRANSITIONS

◄○►

Calisthenics are the exercises used to develop suppleness, coordination, and athletic strength. These elements are necessary in developing the huge trot, deep canter, and fluid transitions seen in the industry's top hunter under saddle horses.

The desired trot comes when the horse has learned to travel at a full stride originating from the power of the hindquarters pushing off. The lift and reach of the shoulders accentuate it, like a person's crawl stroke when swimming. The hunter under saddle horse should lift his shoulders and reach forward with his front legs to achieve maximum extension.

In a deep canter, the horse's shoulders are lifted, creating the space and balance to allow the hind leg to extend well under the belly in a long, deep, forward motion, pushing off with power in each stride. The term "deep-hocked" stems from this movement. From the ground, you can see the hock swing forward under the horse's belly in a long fluid motion of the hind legs.

The canter, a three-beat gait, begins with the outside hind leg driving under and pushing the horse's hindquarters. The inside hock—the one towards the direction of travel—swings forward deep under the belly, and strikes the ground at the same time as the outside front leg. The finishing beat of this gait sequence occurs when the inside front leg extends straight out before hitting the ground. As a rider, you will feel a rise and fall of the horse's hindquarters when he is engaged in a deep canter. This cadence will be easy to ride and will feel smooth. He won't be shuffling his feet behind.

A horse is determined to be traveling on the right or the left lead by which leg is striding further forward at the canter. For instance, if the horse is traveling to the left then he should be on the left lead. This means that both the left front and hind legs are striding further forward than both right legs. The same holds true if the horse is traveling to the right; his right front and hind legs should be striding further forward than his left. Correct leads are important in keeping a horse balanced when traveling in a circle.

Calisthenics are used to develop the strength and coordination necessary to acquire a true slow-legged, three-beat gait. Rhythm, pace, and cadence are critical to a good hunter under saddle canter, which is much like the movement required of the western pleasure horse when loping. The hunter under saddle horse moves in the same deep-hocked manner. Nevertheless, with the specialized tall, Thoroughbred-type horses, more ground is covered with each stride, yet the legs appear to be moving in slow motion.

It's difficult to put a timeline on exactly when to start a young horse on this work. Each horse is an individual and learns and becomes coordinated at his own rate. In general, I start calisthenics and transition work some time between two to four months from the time I started the horse under saddle. I know how to "feel" if he is ready. You might not have ridden enough young horses to have that feel, so here are some guidelines:

A horse should be able to:

- Circle at the walk, trot, and canter in the big arena without having trouble staying on the circle. He shouldn't move his shoulder out or run toward the fence.
- Perform a serpentine at the walk and trot.
- Give to the bit laterally in each direction.

- Correctly execute at least three to four steps in each direction in a turn on the haunches and a turn on the forehand.
- Sidepass easily in each direction while maintaining a straight body.

Varying the Training Sessions

When I start work on calisthenics or transitions, I don't work on one particular move during an entire training session. It is important to give the horse a variety of tasks in a nonroutine manner so he won't recognize patterns and anticipate. Have a lesson plan of what you wish to accomplish in your mind before you begin each session.

A typical workout begins with longeing the horse for about fifteen minutes while saddled, to get his energy level down to the point that he's calm and manageable enough to think rationally. I don't suggest climbing aboard a fresh young horse and going right into a schooling session. Before he goes to the "classroom," it's better that he has had recess time on the longe line first. During longeing, the horse will not wear a bridle—just the halter and longe line. There is no training going on here, just "recess."

After longeing the horse, I bridle him, take him into the arena, then mount and walk him for a few minutes to be sure he is focused on his job. Then I move to the center of the arena and start some trotting serpentines to the right, then the left, and so on—alternating directions. At this stage of training, I still don't ride a horse on the rail, preferring to concentrate my training in the center of the arena doing these exercises, which will build focus and movement.

After a few serpentines, I work the horse on cross-over calisthenics (which will be explained in this chapter). If he crosses his front feet over twice in one direction, I move out of that exercise and into another series of serpentines. From there, I circle the horse. Then, I cross him over in the other direction. Into this random work I mix new concepts, such as the cross-over, with moves he has learned in his foundation work, such as serpentines and circles.

Be sure to longe the horse to get his edge off before you begin work on calisthenics and transitions.

Gear for this Work

After about sixty days under saddle, I ride the horse in some sort of shank bit with a jointed mouthpiece, such as a shank snaffle, when I need extra leverage to encourage the horse to bend his head and neck laterally. It's important that the horse remain light and responsive to the bit. If he becomes heavy or dull in the mouth, this work quickly becomes a pulling contest. A leverage bit also works to supple and soften the mouth.

At the same time I ask for the lateral bend, I'm careful to watch his head position and attitude. If he shows that he's timid by backing away from the bit and moving his chin down toward his chest, I need to switch him to "less bit," but something that will still prevent a pulling contest. A twisted wire snaffle is a good choice for this task.

Calisthenics to Develop the Trot

The following calisthenics work well in teaching a horse to move with his shoulders lifted, and develop that "swimmer's crawl stroke" reach in the trot:

Circles and Serpentines:

Before this point you used circles and serpentines to gain control over your horse's speed and direction. With those basics instilled, you can now use circles and serpentines to provide your horse with an awareness of how to use his shoulders, which will prepare him for moving in self-carriage.

A horse should not drop his shoulders and dive into the center of a circle. It looks and feels clumsy. His shoulders should ideally be up and his body bent from his nose through his shoulders, rib cage, and hips to his tail, in a nice balanced arc that mirrors the shape of the circle.

To work a circle to the right, hold the right rein slightly shorter than the left. At the same time, add light pressure on your left rein to restrict your horse from bending his neck too far into the direction of the circle. When he was learning to follow his nose, moves were exaggerated so he could get the idea. If his head were pulled far to the right, he would follow it. But now that he understands this basic concept, less bend is needed. His lateral head and neck position will be subtle, in line with the arc of his body. Pressure from the outside (left) leg just behind the girth encourages forward motion and maintains the balance of the arc. Use slight pressure with the inside (right) calf at the girth area to bend the horse around your leg for the desired arc. This leg aid will also keep the horse moving forward between the bridle and your legs, encouraging him to keep his shoulders up so he doesn't dive into the center of the circle.

Ride one or two rotations of a circle and then change to a serpentine to mix things up. Return to circles in the opposite direction.

Serpentines now become a reminder to the horse to keep his shoulders up. Let me first explain what a dropped shoulder feels like, then how to work serpentines to correct it.

Try this human exercise away from the horse. Lift and pull back your right shoulder, then walk in a small circle to the right. Feel how you're able to sweep in a graceful move with each step, like a dancer. Now, keeping your arm close to your side, lower your right shoulder as far down as you can, and lean into your circle. Walk another circle to the right. Feel like a klutz? Are your steps clumsy, short, and uncoordinated? Feels awful, doesn't it? Now, if you had someone there to remind you to lift that shoulder, you would travel more like a dancer than a jackhammer. That's the difference you will feel with your horse.

Let's say you are riding in a serpentine to the right, and feel your horse drop his shoulder. As soon as you feel it, change directions by sending him into a serpentine to the left. If he drops his shoulder in the left serpentine, change directions and move him to the right. He will learn that he must keep his shoulders lifted in order to stay balanced.

Your hands must remain soft and smooth when changing directions in the serpentines and circles. Avoid using quick, jerking hand motions that will unbalance the horse's head and neck and cause him to fall into the new direction. The intent is not to unbalance the horse to the point that he throws his head up in the air and forgets he is wearing a bridle. Using your hands slowly and smoothly will allow the horse time to reposition his body's bend and transition smoothly into the new direction of travel. Ideally, he will drop down into the bridle and relax his neck down and into the arc of the circle. This position is referred to as a "lateral position off the inside shoulder." As he bends and laterally drops his neck, release him to a loose rein. This lateral neck work during serpentines and circles will set him up for the headset work that I will explain in the chapter on "finishing."

Cross-Over Exercise

The cross-over exercise is a great aid in teaching a horse how to reach out with his shoulders. For a cross-over to the right, bend the horse to the left in a counter arc. While either walking or in a medium sitting trot in a circle to the right, press your left leg against his rib cage. Draw your right rein back toward your right thigh to help move the shoulders to the right. The horse should cross his left front leg over his right front leg while maintaining forward motion. This is a similar exercise to the shoulder-in maneuver in dressage.

When asking for a cross-over to the left, the cues are just the opposite from above.

Begin this calisthenic first at the walk. Reward your horse after one or two crossing steps by releasing him out of the cross-over and letting him move into a circle in the direction toward which his body is bent. For example, if you are doing a cross-over exercise to the right, his body is counter-arced to the left; simply release him into a left circle for his reward. Then you can cross-over the other way, or add more crossing steps. Once your horse figures out the

Coming out of a left serpentine, starting one to the right.

As I prepare to serpentine to the right, I apply direct rein pressure with my right hand. The indirect (left) rein held with a little pressure against this mare's neck keeps her from overbending her head and neck to the right. Pressure from my right (inside) calf will arc her around my leg. She has correctly moved her head and neck laterally toward the point of her right shoulder.

Cross-over calisthenic to the left, at the walk. The horse is counter-arced to the opposite direction of the cross-over. She is arced to the right, but is being asked to cross her right front foot over her left as she steps to the left.

mechanics of this exercise, you can move into a sitting trot and repeat this calisthenic. Remember, it is important to do equal work in both directions.

Whenever you feel either shoulder drop, immediately lift that shoulder into another cross-over exercise in the opposite direction.

Canter Calisthenics

These exercises will help to develop the desired deep canter.

The Trot-to-Canter Calisthenic

Up until now you have been putting your horse into a canter from a trot. This exercise expands on that concept while you convey to your horse that the canter depart should originate in the hindquarters. By teaching a horse to step off into the canter beginning from his hindquarters, you educate him on rocking his weight back onto his hindquarters so that the first step into the canter is a push from the rear, rather than a pull from the front end. This is preferable because it tightens up the walk-to-canter transition by eliminating any unwanted trot steps. It also engages the horse's hocks for the desired canter frame.

Start by trotting a fifty-foot circle in a medium sitting trot. Gently bump his mouth with the reins until he gives to the bit. Even though the goal is not to develop a headset, overexaggerate an extra low head carriage by seesawing the horse's mouth. By heavily engaging the horse into the bridle and exaggerating the roundness of the horse's back, his only choice is to stride deeper under his belly with his hocks. Bump his sides with your legs to help him suck up his stomach and round his back. Drive him into the bit with your legs, and then ask him to canter off with a vocal command (kissing sound) and outside leg pressure.

Ideally, he will move right into the canter in a deep-hocked motion. His first step into the canter will be from his hindquarters. If he stays round in his back and deep with his hock through the transition, release rein pressure and allow him to canter for one or two rotations of the circle.

If he throws his head up in the air to escape the bridle, or hollows his back and elevates his forehand while transitioning into the canter, return to the sitting trot. Repeat your hand and leg aids to put him into a frame. Don't ask for the transition into the canter until his head is down, his back is round, and his hocks are engaged to reach up under his belly for a hindquarters push into the canter. This engagement will feel like you are sitting atop a round ball. The horse will feel like he is pushing you forward into the canter rather than pulling heavily onto his forehand and falling forward through the transition.

Repeat this exercise several times until the horse begins to find his own frame by balancing his weight back for a hindquarters-push canter departure.

This calisthenic is designed to educate your horse on how the canter departure should originate. It is not intended for work on

At the sitting trot, I ask her to cross-over to the right by counter-arcing her to the left . . .

. . . and she crosses over with her left front foot.

In the trot-to-canter calisthenic, I bump the horse's mouth to obtain an exaggerated, low head carriage and create a "block" of the horse's front end. That makes her round her back and move deeper under her belly with her hock.

speed control or headsets. Too much work with his head held in an excessively low head carriage will cause the horse to balance too much weight on his forehand, therefore dropping his shoulders down instead of lifting them up.

Backup Cross-Over Calisthenic – "C-ing" the Horse

This exercise works on pace and cadence. When the horse is easily able to pick up the canter as a result of the trot-to-canter calisthenic, we must begin to make him rock back onto his haunches, lift his shoulders, and stay in the proper canter frame. Backing up the horse distributes the weight onto his hindquarters and lightens the forehand so that he can easily lift his shoulders. Arcing his body into the direction of the desired lead prepares his body for the proper carriage in the canter. This carriage is what produces the slow-legged, deep-hocked canter of a winning hunter under saddle horse.

Ask the horse to canter off by using your vocal command (kissing sound) and outside leg aid. As soon as he starts to lean forward onto his forehand and pull himself into the canter, stop him and back him up. You will now set him up to restart, using the backup cross-over calisthenic to position his body. Here are the steps to this positioning for cantering off again on the right lead.

As you back the horse up, lift his right shoulder by raising your right rein and laying it against his neck. Apply pressure with your right leg at the girth to move his shoulders to the left. He will cross-over his right front leg in front of his left as he lifts his shoulders. This places his body in the shape of a letter C. I call it "C-ing" the horse. His body arcs to the right with his nose tipped right, his shoulders lifted to the outside of the arc, and his right shoulder is up. His hip is tipped to the inside of the arc, to the right.

This position tells the horse, "This is the position I want your body to maintain while you are cantering, so let's try it again." Of course, you won't hold him in an exaggerated C when you show him, but you will still want a slight arc. In addition, this is the beginning of your horse's education on self-carriage.

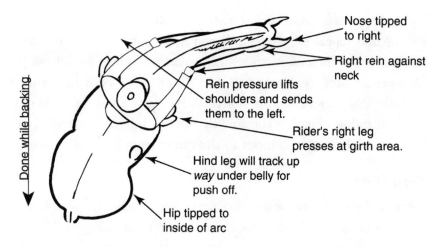

Nose tipped to right

Right rein against neck

Rein pressure lifts shoulders and sends them to the left.

Rider's right leg presses at girth area.

Hind leg will track up *way* under belly for push off.

Hip tipped to inside of arc

Done while backing.

This arc is for a right lead canter depart.

Backup cross-over calisthenic – "C-ing" the horse.

During schooling, when the horse is in a C to the right, I allow him to move forward by keeping his nose tipped slightly to the right. If he dives in that direction, I ask him to cross-over to the left at a walk to remind him that I want his right shoulder to remain lifted. Once he moves forward and is keeping that shoulder lifted, I cue him for a canter by using my voice command (kiss) and outside (left) leg pressure to squeeze him into the canter. At first, he might want to trot forward instead of cantering off. If he does so, I stop him and use the backup cross-over C again, then cue him again for the canter, repeating the procedure until he does a correct canter departure. It might take several attempts before he masters this skill.

Do this exercise across the arena and away from the rail in straight lines rather than circles. Working straight lines instead of circles creates a true lead cue rather than the horse picking a lead based on which direction he is circling.

In the beginning, ask for only two to four canter strides after each departure. The idea is to obtain quality of stride rather than quantity. After the two to four strides, bring him back to a stop using the "whoa" command rather than hard rein pressure. Back him up and repeat the exercise. When he responds in a calm manner and holds those few strides in a balanced frame, verbally stop him, pat his neck as a reward, and let him rest for a few moments.

I use this exercise on my horses forever. It's great for building strength and flexibility. It consistently works on shoulder carriage, as well as on initiating transitions to the canter from the stop or walk.

Transitions

A big factor that determines whether or not a young horse is ready for transitions and finish work centers around his strength. Moves like the canter departure are tough and require strength. If your young horse struggles to perform these moves, he might not be physically capable and will need to continue working on foundation exercises such as beginner circles and serpentines before he starts the more difficult moves. A rider must understand that it takes time for a horse to build the muscles necessary to perform this work, the precise time determined by whether you have a young strong horse or a gangly one that still needs work and time.

The horse's state of mind also enters into the picture. A fractious young horse is probably confused and not mentally ready for this work. He might show it by kicking out at your leg pressure, nervously anticipating every move, resisting heavily in the bridle, or nervously chomping the bit. These are indications that he needs to remain at his current level and not proceed to more challenging tasks. But if he is calm and accepting, he is ready to move on to the next training level. Let your horse's behavior tell you when to challenge him and when to retreat to previously mastered maneuvers.

Proper transitions are critical in the show pen. If you get a good transition, you will have a good gait. If the transition is poor, you'll spend 90% of the time on the rail trying to repair the damage and attempting to rebalance your horse into the correct frame. And just about the time you get that accomplished, the announcer will call for another transition!

The calisthenics in this chapter are instrumental in teaching a horse to carry out smooth transitions. They teach him to use his body correctly by engaging his hindquarters and lifting his shoulders. This weight transfer is required for a successful departure transition into any gait.

Which Transitions Will Your Horse Need to Know?

The judge determines which transitions will be asked for in the show pen. It's as simple as that. Judges who have consideration for young, green horses are inclined to ask for transitions that they know young horses can handle. This is especially true at the start of the show year when a judge is viewing a Green Hunter Under Saddle class and knows it's the first show for many of these youngsters. Often, a judge will call for a walk transition between the trot and the canter; he knows it is difficult for a young horse to go from a forward long-strided trot into a rocked-back canter, and maintain the proper canter pace and cadence. So, the sympathetic judge calls for the horses to go from the trot down to the walk, which settles a young green horse and keeps him thinking, "down," with his pace, instead of "I have to go faster!" The judge will then call for the canter.

Smaller shows usually require less challenging transitions, but at a major show such as the All-American Quarter Horse Congress held in October, many of the horses will have more classes under their belts. They're all pretty high caliber as well as seasoned, so judges (there will be more than one officiating in each class) might call for the young horses to trot on the rail, then pick up the canter, then go down to a walk. They'll reverse the class for the second direction and have them canter, then transition down to the trot, and finish the class at the walk. Then the horses will be asked to stop and back on the rail, or come to the center to demonstrate their ability to back up. These can be challenging transitions for a young, green horse, but something he'll need to know as a seasoned show horse.

The walk-to-canter transition is probably easier for a young horse to handle mentally, but physically it isn't a piece of cake. A young horse might not yet be strong enough to really push off from behind while maintaining a level and correct topline. Or he'll rock back and drop his weight onto his haunches, but he won't round his back. His head will move way up in the air, and he'll look a little awkward in the neck, especially if he's a long-necked Thoroughbred type. A giraffe-length neck rolled into an accordion position, because the horse is trying to get his feet underneath him to canter off, is not a pretty picture. That contortion proves that this is a tough transition physically for a growthy young horse that is long and stretchy. The solution: more calisthenics to strengthen his topline.

Even though some of the work in this chapter will ultimately lead to a headset—which is the result of engagement of the hindquarters, rounding of the back, and lifting of the shoulders—the next chapter will explain the development of the desired head and neck position. That work belongs in the last actual training chapter. Years ago people began locking horses' heads down during the first sessions in the round pen, using gimmicks such as "armpit" lines run around the horse's body, then up between the front legs and attached to the bit. The horse's head was pulled straight down, and the lines tugged on alternate corners of the mouth each time the horse took a step. Then when the horse was ready to ride, other gimmicks were used to keep his head "set" right from the start. As I've explained, that's not my approach. A young horse might move his head in the air during transitions and calisthenics work because he physically needs it there to lift his shoulders to perform these new tasks. As he strengthens his topline, he will be able to round his body and lower his head and neck.

Establishing shoulder control is important now. So are teaching the young horse to travel deep-hocked, and showing him how he can step into transitions by using his hindquarters. Don't sweat the headset yet. As long as your horse gives to the bit when you pick up on the reins, you are right on track.

Using Calisthenics to Improve the Canter Departure

In both the round pen and in the big arena, a young horse begins his foundation for the canter departure by trotting into it. When I trot a horse into the canter, I use quite a bit of contact on the bridle. At the same time, I use my legs to encourage him to round his back and drive off from behind. I put him into a medium sitting trot, then when he canters off at my request I release the rein pressure. This is the foundation a young horse needs to successfully learn the walk-to-canter transition.

The backup cross-over calisthenic is ideal for teaching this transition. Although this exercise originates from a stop, once the young horse realizes the rider's voice and leg cue connection, it will be easy for him to associate the cues even from the walk. Then after being cued to canter, the horse will start to rock back and engage his hock for a canter departure on his own.

Some people try to teach this transition without the foundation. Out of the blue they say, "Hey, horse, we have a show next weekend and you need to learn how to pick up the canter from the walk—now!" The result is a horse that charges off into the canter. The rider jerks on the reins to slow the horse down. Then each time the horse is asked to canter, he anticipates getting jerked around. He gets frustrated and nervous. There are no positive experiences in the past that he can build from to gain the confidence necessary for a smooth and relaxed canter departure.

The trot-to-canter calisthenic is also helpful in establishing the desired level topline as the horse pushes off into the canter. I use this calisthenic to rid the transition of the initial head lift that is typically seen from too much pulling down and backing up. And I'll use the backup cross-over calisthenic to keep the horse's weight shifted back onto his haunches. This prevents him from getting too much weight onto his forehand, which can be the drawback of the trot-to-canter transition if it is overused.

Every positive training technique carries with it a negative consequence. For example, pulling your horse down to a stop and backing him up to correct a poor canter departure can encourage the horse to become reluctant to move into the transition. Therefore, you need another training technique, such as the backup cross-over calisthenic, to correct this new problem. Be aware of the possible problems that you could be creating and counteract them quickly by keeping things varied. Most of the time, it is the rider who has created the problems he or she is trying to deal with. By analyzing your riding skills and training goals, you will be better able to understand where your horse's problems are arising from.

Walk-to-Canter Transition

When I am preparing to show a horse or actually showing in a class, my walk-to-canter transitions are as follows (with this example moving to the right): When the announcer asks for a canter, I supple the horse's face by softly wiggling my fingers on the reins and sink my weight into the saddle to draw the horse's attention to the upcoming cue. For the voice command, I make a kissing noise. I use my left (outside) leg to pressure the horse's left rib cage. At the same time, I draw in softly on my right rein to remind the horse to lift his right shoulder and frame into the "C'd-up" body carriage. He will then step off from his hindquarters and depart into a soft canter.

During practice sessions, anything other than this ideal departure is disciplined with a backup cross-over exercise or the trot-to-canter calisthenic.

Walk-to-Trot Transition

This transition is not difficult. By this time, the horse's foundation work has been walk, trot, then into the canter. When showing a horse on a walk-to-trot transition, I use my voice to make a "cluck" sound. I use different voice commands for different gaits so that the horse will have an easier time distinguishing between cues. I then lightly squeeze or bump both my legs against the horse's sides. My hands work to supple the horse's face so that he'll move into the bridle and maintain a flat topline. As his trot gait is established I begin to post on the correct diagonal.

Trot-to-Canter Transition

After the horse graduates to calisthenics and transition work I rarely return to the beginning method of getting him to canter from the trot. A few days before a show, I will practice the trot-to-canter transition a time or two just to remind us both that we can still do it. However, I don't ask for this transition very often at home because I don't want the horse breaking into a canter while I am trying to extend his trot stride. I want to push for length of stride in the trot without that threat of getting a canter instead. It's wonderful to feel a horse advanced in his training striding out with a strong, floaty trot, and to know he's going to stay there unless you tell him otherwise. However, if he's anticipating that you'll ask for a canter, he won't give his all in the trot department.

My solution to this potential problem, on those few occasions when I do ask for a trot-to-canter departure, is to slow down the horse's trot stride and bring him back to me by softening and slowing my post, which in turn helps him to distribute his weight back onto his haunches. I then ask him to canter off with the same cue I used from the walk. This produces a much prettier transition than "chasing" him into the canter from the trot. A horse that is chased into the canter quickens and builds his trot stride, then essentially breaks gait into the canter. He travels too far on his forehand, and his hock won't be deep up under his body. The canter gait must then be repaired because of this poor transition.

Canter-to-Trot Transition

This is another transition that I don't practice a lot. I just need to know I can get it when I ask for it. If the horse has mastered his upward transitions and also has a good mastery of what "whoa" means, this downward transition shouldn't be a problem.

I ask for the trot with a voice command—quietly saying "trot"—and then relaxing my seat. I fiddle with the reins, which acts as a wake-up call to focus the horse's attention to the voice command. Because of his "whoa" training, a young horse might first slow down abruptly, almost to a stop. In this case I follow up my "trot" voice command with a cluck, and instantly send him forward with pressure from my legs. Then I pet him to let him know he did well with this new transition, which is easy to teach if the horse has a clear understanding of the "whoa" voice command. He will tune in to the fact that hearing your voice speak a word in a firm tone means he is to stop. Softening your voice to say "trot" quietly modifies the down transition to a trot instead of a stop. It's a matter of degree.

Canter-to-Walk Transition

This transition is easy for a horse that has a good "whoa" foundation. As you canter your horse and are ready to make the downward transition, say "walk," which at first sounds like "whoa" to a horse. Relax your seat and sit down in the saddle. When the horse sets down almost to a stop, apply pressure with your legs to move him into a walk. Use your hands to maintain a stable topline.

THE UPS AND DOWNS OF POSTING

- **Posting on the Correct Diagonal:** Posting the trot makes riding this gait more comfortable, especially when increasing stride. There is an old saying that works well to explain the concept of posting, or rising to the trot, on the correct diagonal: "Rise and fall with the leg on the wall." An explanation of how a horse trots is also a great help in understanding the process.

  The trot is a two-beat diagonal gait, meaning that the diagonal pair of legs—right front and left hind—hit the ground at the same time. Posting on the correct diagonal is necessary to help the horse maintain balance of stride, particularly in corners. In order to post on the correct diagonal, use the outside front leg as the guide. As that leg goes to the ground and the horse's outside shoulder is moving back toward your own outside leg, you should be seated. As the outside leg lifts off the ground and the shoulder moves forward, you rise out of your saddle. As you become advanced in your hunt-seat riding, you will reach a point where it is no longer necessary to look down for your correct diagonal. You will find it through feel.

• **Softening the Post:** "Softening"means that you are no longer posting to send your horse forward, but are slowing down your post by softening the intensity of the rise in order to cue the horse to come back to your seat and roll back onto his haunches. Softening the post helps a rider slow the horse's legs at a trot if the horse becomes too quick-legged. It is also beneficial to soften the post in order to collect the trot, before entering a canter departure.

{ 9 }

FINISH WORK
AND HEADSET

———◄O►———

When a horse is demonstrating consistency with calisthenics and transitions, you can begin concentrating on finishing work with such show pen requirements as head and neck position, rhythm, cadence, fluid motion, and that all-important self-carriage.

There are no shortcuts or timelines for this work. There will never be a time while you are showing when you can say, "We're done. I'll never have to train this horse again." Your horse is an athlete and requires training for the duration of his show career. Finish work will often be combined with a return to foundation concepts, such as circles, serpentines, calisthenics, and transitions. Continued use of calisthenics will also help your horse establish consistency in movement.

Don't look at finishing work as an endless task, but rather a chance for you as a horseman to build on your ability to produce a winner. Just because a basketball player has made the pro ranks doesn't mean he will never again practice the fundamentals of dribbling or free throws.

While this chapter addresses a number of aspects on finishing, arranged in specific categories for clarity, the same concept of mixing things up must still be applied. Don't work on the same moves for an entire session. Your horse must continue to wait for your cues and not anticipate.

Now is the time when you can finally work on the rail, but there should be no monotonous round-and-round schooling. The horse should view going to the rail as a reward. As this chapter shows, I let a horse travel on the rail after he does and maintains his gait correctly. You'll also see that I don't use any set pattern to determine how long he travels there. I might take him to the rail at the canter for fifteen to twenty strides, then return to the center to do a calisthenic exercise. When we go back to the rail the next time, it might be for just five strides. Then I will stop him and let him stand as a reward.

I don't think in terms of gradually increasing the number of strides on the rail, but we may eventually travel all the way around the arena if the horse's pace, rhythm, and cadence stay correct. But at this current stage of training, I know I can easily guide the horse with control over his forward, backward, and sideways movements. Where we perform these maneuvers, on or off the rail, is just a matter of location. The important thing is that wherever the horse is asked to work, he must still think about me and wonder when I will stop him and let him rest on the rail. That way he will never associate the rail with speeding. This is important to establish, because when I'm at a show I want my horse to be thinking "stop" rather than "go." I want to have to push him around the pen with my legs, rather than having to work at slowing him down.

Elements of Finishing Work

Preparing to Work With Less Warm-Up Time

In previous work, longeing your horse before riding to reduce energy levels was standard practice. However, at shows you won't always have a lot of time for a warm-up. You'll have to ride into a class "cold" or just not as warmed-up as you'd like, and it might be on a three-year-old that has trouble focusing. So, as you begin your finishing work, start to wean your horse from preride longeing. I usually do this during the summer when it's hot and horses aren't as invigorated as they are when the air is cold and crisp. I decrease longeing time gradually over several days until I finally climb on the horse for the first time with absolutely no preride longeing time. This doesn't mean that I'll never again longe before I ride. I just want to experiment with a "cold ride" so that I can anticipate the behavior of a young horse when the routine is broken.

Working on the Show Pen Walk

The walk should be an even four-beat gait, relaxed and evenly paced. The horse should not show hesitation between each step, nor should he be walking extremely quickly. The excessive slow walk with prolonged hesitation between each step can be considered a break of gait. The extremely fast walk will make the horse appear nervous. Plan on schooling your horse for a relaxed walking speed that falls between these extremes. To help establish an idea of the proper pace, watch a few hunter under saddle classes to see the walking pace done by the winners.

I spend about five to ten percent of each ride working on the walk. Along with stopping, standing, and allowing the horse to relax, the walk helps a horse understand that his routine isn't totally made up of trotting and cantering. There are times when I ask the horse to walk in a relaxed manner in between trot or canter departures. If he is not anticipating the upward transition and walks calmly, I know his walk won't be a problem. But if he does not want to walk at an acceptable pace and seems nervous, or he is obviously trying to start a transition before I ask, it's time for more quiet walk schooling. I stop and back him, then walk him off four or five steps and stop and back again, repeating the process until he understands that he is to walk quietly and is almost anticipating the stop. Stopping and backing should be done with finesse rather than anger. To jerk him to a stop and haul him back would increase his nervousness.

It helps to reverse directions often during this schooling, so the horse doesn't think he's getting closer to arriving somewhere in particular, especially the gate.

Perfecting the Trot

The ideal is to produce a horse that is slow-legged and has a long reach to his stride. The movement almost appears to be in slow motion, even though it covers a great deal of ground. On a horse that is fast-legged, one whose legs are moving quickly and taking short strides, you feel as though you're riding a Shetland pony that is scurrying along. But when a hunter under saddle horse is covering the ground with a long stride, it feels as though he is spending some hang time, dwelling in the air. And while there is something of an increase in speed when the horse really lengthens his stride, his steps are not quick. He is moving long and low across the ground.

You'll need to work on slowing the legs before you can get the reach. Let's say your horse is traveling quick-legged in a fast-strided trot, feeling as though any moment he will break into a canter. He is "traveling ahead of your leg," which makes you feel like you need to post ninety miles per hour to keep up with him. You might worry that if you apply leg aids now, your horse will speed up even more or break into the canter. The first step in correcting this is to use the sitting trot to bring the horse down into a slower, more collected trot.

Rather than posting, sit down into the saddle. Move to the center of the arena and apply rein pressure to bring the horse back to your seat and legs. This reminds him that your legs are used to help him establish pace and cadence, and he is not to speed away from them. Bump your legs against his sides and put him into serpentines and cross-over exercises at the sitting trot.

Once the horse is relaxed and trotting with the rhythm of your legs instead of ahead of them, resume posting. If he remains in rhythm with your legs, apply more pressure by squeezing your calves against the horse's rib cage when you are in the "down" position of posting. Release them when you are on the "up" move.

When riding at the sitting trot stay down in the saddle and do not post.

This pumping motion encourages a longer stride, but be sure the stride is indeed lengthening, not that his legs are getting faster. If he does get fast-legged again, go back to the sitting trot and again establish control.

Once you feel that the horse is relaxed and moving in a smooth and proper cadence, reward him by taking him out to the rail or near it, and let him travel along the rail for a few strides. But if he speeds up again, take him back to the center and repeat the serpentines and circles.

When you take the horse to the rail and round the corner on the short side of the arena, you might feel him drop his shoulder. It will feel as though he is diving into the turn and cutting the corner. Instantly correct this with cross-over exercises at the trot. There are two places you can do so, both equally effective. You can trot him right to the center of the arena and start the cross-overs there. Or, you can move the horse off the rail about fifteen or twenty feet, and the next time you feel his shoulder drop you can do a cross-over toward the rail away from the direction that he just dropped his shoulder. For example, if he cut his corner to the left, cross him over to the right. Keep his head bent to the left with direct-rein pressure, and maintain very light indirect rein to move his shoulders toward the rail. At the same time, you will use your left leg to apply pressure to his side. He should cross his left front leg over the right, which will lift the dropped left shoulder.

Think of this as a leg yield toward the rail. A leg yield consists of moving forward and sideways at the same time, on a diagonal with the horse's body counterarched (bent away from the direction of travel). This position lifts the horse's inside shoulder and reinforces that he must keep that shoulder lifted in the corners of the arena.

Once a horse learns this move, he will remember it, and you can use it as a preventive measure during the show. If you are worried that he'll drop his inside shoulder on a corner at the end of the arena, you can move his shoulders over toward the rail as you begin to enter the corner, or anytime you feel his shoulders dive in during the turn. Before you get to the corner, pull back lightly on your inside rein and add inside leg pressure. This will "stand up" his shoulders, and he'll keep them lifted as he rounds the turn.

Striving for a Deeper, Consistent Canter

When a horse is engaged in a deep canter, his shoulders are lifted so that his inside hock, the one that comes further forward because of his lead, can extend well under his belly. He takes a long, deep step behind with each stride of the canter as his hind leg swings forward. He travels deep-hocked, which means that when his hind leg comes that far under his belly, his hindquarters become "engaged" and act as the driver. He pushes himself around the arena, rather than pulling himself with his front end.

He feels slow-legged and smooth because he is elevating his shoulders properly. This shoulder elevation leaves the path clear for his hind leg to move quite far forward. The push is concentrated from the hindquarters, so his front legs are not lifted in a marching motion. Instead, they move close to the ground and flat-kneed in a very "sweeping" look.

Ideally, the horse's hindquarters lift upward with each stride. The rider should have no trouble feeling this rise and fall. If there is no lift in the hindquarters, the horse is shuffling or "four-beating," which is undesirable. A proper canter is a three-beat gait. On the left lead, beat one occurs when the outside (right) hind leg hits the ground. Both shoulders should be lifted. Beat two occurs when the inside (left) hock swings through and reaches deeply under the horse's belly. The inside hind leg and outside front leg move at the same time, striking the ground in unison. The conclusion of beat two causes the top of the horse's hip to lift upward as the canter sequence is completed by beat three. This third beat occurs when the inside front (left) leg extends forward, striking the ground well in front of the horse. The greater the engagement of the hindquarters, the more lift through the shoulders. This results in a greater extension of the horse's front legs, which also creates the flat knee we want to see in a hunter under saddle horse.

Along with engagement, we strive to produce a horse that travels with rhythm and cadence, which together produce fluid motion. Watch a successful finished hunter under saddle horse move around the show pen, and you can compare his movement to that of a dancer. The cadence is his footfall pattern. The rhythm is the beat at which his steps are carried out. For example, you can visualize the rhythm of waltz steps at the canter—one, two, three; one, two, three; one, two, three. Such a horse appears to float effortlessly around the pen. He looks pleasurable to ride, and the rider appears to just sit quietly in the saddle and enjoy the trip.

A consistent horse maintains the same pace and rhythm all the way around the pen, demonstrating how truly broke he is. He hits the same lick each time. He moves like a Lexus on cruise control.

An inconsistent horse might take one deep stride behind, then a couple of short, choppy strides. He looks more like a stick-shift car with a bad clutch. This problem is often seen in horses that are green or just not as broke as the Lexus-type horses. A green horse may have the talent of a champion, but still lack the consistency needed to finish at the top of the class. His finish work will eventually bring out his talent and ability.

The canter calisthenics explained in Chapter 8 should be continued. When combined with more advanced moves, they will help establish and maintain rhythm, pace, cadence, and consistency.

One advanced move is the counter-canter, which should be done in circles and serpentines. A horse needs to be well-broke, with a solid foundation of the basics, and a mastery of the calisthenics and transitions, and with the physical strength to tackle something this demanding. He should also know his leads well, and have the necessary coordination to attempt this exercise.

To put it simply, when you ask a horse to counter-canter, you intentionally put him on the "wrong" lead. If he's moving left, he is on the right lead, and vice versa. Your horse might need more rein and leg pressure than usual, both to convince him to work this way and to balance his head, neck, and body in the process.

Start this exercise by putting your horse on the right lead at the canter in a circle, or the right curve of a serpentine. Ride him in a straight line for a stride or two. Then, use strong left rein and left leg pressure to arc his body to the left, but still maintain the right lead. His head, neck, and body will be bent to the left, as you now ask him to circle to that direction. What you're after is the use of centrifugal force to swing the horse's hip and hindquarters to the outside of the circle. After making the left circle, come back to a right circle again. The horse will be well-engaged, with his hind end propelling his movement. Work in that circle on the "correct" lead, then serpentine or circle him again to the left on the counter lead.

This exercise strengthens the horse so that he can better engage his hip and hock. It will increase the amount of swing of the inside hind lead leg, forward and deep under his belly. When you first begin this exercise, just ask for two or three strides on the counter lead. As the horse's strength increases, increase the number of strides in the counter-canter. Because it is difficult at first, some horses will try to switch back to the "correct" lead. This is nothing to worry about. Just bring the horse back down to the trot, then restart the canter on the lead you want and continue the exercise. At first it will be easier for the horse to do this work if your circles and serpentines are wider than what you've generally ridden. You can narrow the size of the circles or serpentines as the horse feels more coordinated. Even though he appears gawky at first, he will be gaining strength and flexibility.

With an advanced horse that is accustomed to counter-cantering, this exercise can also be used to loosen stiff shoulder and neck muscles if he tends to carry his head behind the vertical, from poll to nose. Narrowing the serpentine and swinging the horse's neck laterally from side to side will unlock his withers area and loosen tight neck and shoulder muscles. As a result, he will be able to surf his neck out in front of himself in a relaxed manner.

This is also a great exercise for developing pace and cadence, as well as tuning up a horse that has been shown a few times and has a lazy canter because the novelty of the show pen has worn off.

The half halt is another exercise that collects and engages the hock and rounds the back. In a sense, it is like the backup cross-over calisthenic, but is done with forward motion. When I ask for a half halt, I ride the horse at the canter in a straight line, then I simultaneously use pressure on the reins and solid leg pressure, with more pressure from my outside leg, to squeeze the horse forward and lift and round his back. The horse knows by this stage of training that he is to give to the bridle. Carrying his head a little high is fine, because what I am really after is an exaggerated lift in the shoulders.

This exercise blocks the horse's forward motion, exaggerates the lift of his shoulders, and increases depth of hock. Lifting the shoulders rebalances the horse so that he really rocks his weight back onto his hocks. You will feel this rocked-back motion and the increased length of hind leg stride. And because the back legs are coming up under the horse in extremely long steps, the canter will feel as though it is in slow motion. When I feel this effect, I relax the intense leg and rein pressure, and allow the horse to move forward without restriction.

During this exercise, a rider must sit deep in the saddle. This is a big factor, because if you're not sitting down through your seat, one of three things will happen: (1) you will pull the horse down to a stop; (2) you won't achieve the desired depth of hock; or (3) the horse will break down into a trot. This exercise is, in essence, exactly what we didn't want to do when the horse was first learning to canter: step on the brake (the reins) and while pushing on the accelerator (the rider's legs.) By now, the horse has come a long way in his training, and can accept this contradiction of cues, and by doing so exaggerate the lift of the shoulders to increase the swing and depth of his hock. This exercise can be done for a short time every day as needed but as with the other exercises, calisthenics, and transitions, it should not constitute an entire session by itself. Continue to mix the old with the new, returning often to calisthenics and transition work. As you mix and match exercises in this manner, you can start adding some cantering time on the rail. The secret is to consistently analyze your horse and his progress, then develop a daily lesson plan to build on his strengths and improve upon his weaknesses. For example, some days you may work more on transitions, while other days you may need more work on cadence.

Let's say I am in the center of the arena working on a canter departure. The horse not only performs it well, but stays in the canter for fifteen to twenty strides without changing pace or cadence. Before I stop the horse I take him to the rail and let him canter along the rail for a few more strides, as a reward to him for what he has just accomplished with his quality canter. We travel up the rail, and if the pace and cadence are still consistent, we continue around the corner at the short end of the arena. I then ask him to stop, reward him by petting his neck, and let him rest for a few moments. Once the rest is over, I ask for the backup cross-over exercise to put him into the C position for the lead I'm working on. I ask for a canter departure that heads away from the rail and across the middle of the arena. If the transition is good and the horse holds a steady canter for several strides after, it's all right to drift back to the rail. But if he is incorrect in his reaction, I take immediate action.

For example, if the horse throws his head up in the air during a transition, I interrupt that transition and move him in a trot to the center of the arena where I put him into circles and serpentines, overexaggerating his headset with extra rein pressure. This correction causes him to round his back and get into a good frame. Then I ask for a canter departure, reminding him that the departure must originate from the hindquarters; although I want him to lift his shoulders, his head and neck should not come up.

Establishing Consistent Head and Neck Carriage

You're probably saying, "Hooray! This is the part I've been waiting for!" But you should also know that it was important that you did, indeed, wait until your horse had several months under saddle before starting this work. That is because the desired headset and neck carriage come from good movement. A horse that engages his hindquarters, rounds his back, and lifts his shoulders will move with a relaxed head and neck. He'll move in a balanced frame with his neck stretched out to produce the much sought-after level topline that extends from his poll or the tip of his ears across the top of his neck to the withers, and then across to the top of his hip.

The horse's face should be slightly in front of, or on, the vertical. His chin should not be drawn back toward his chest. Had you started this work too early or forced the headset with gimmicks, your horse would have already assumed that intimidated "chin-to-chest" posture, and proper movement would have been sacrificed.

Now that you've allowed him to learn to use his body correctly and he's working well at all three gaits, the training required to keep his head and neck where they belong won't be an overwhelming task.

Before starting, I want to explain the term "headset," which is deceiving to many people. It is a phrase that has been used for decades, and for years it was thought that the only way to accomplish this was to force the horse to flex at the poll and "set his head." But a rider should strive to teach the horse to lower his neck from the withers and use his neck as a tool for acquiring balance, while maintaining a round back. The level topline that occurs as a result of proper training actually consists of a rounded arch that goes from the poll to the top of the hip, with the highest point being the roundness of the lifted back. You can see from the ground that a horse in this sort of frame has lifted shoulders and is balanced over his hocks. From the saddle, you recognize that your horse is giving at the withers rather than the poll because his neck is lowered, lengthened forward, and relaxed.

This photo of Blanche trotting illustrates the correct topline: a rounded arch that goes from the poll right to the top of the hip, with the highest point being the roundness of the lifted back. The photo is also a good example of a horse in self-carriage.

But if a horse is only giving at the poll, his neck will look like an accordion. He will be overflexed, with very little drop in the elevation of his neck. A horse that positions himself in this manner appears to be intimidated and afraid of the bridle. As a trainer and judge, that's the last thing I want to see in a hunter under saddle horse.

While a rider's hands were once considered the only aid to produce a "headset," the truth is that much of the proper position of the horse's head and neck is a result of a rider correctly using his or her legs. When you wrap your legs around a horse, it encourages him to pull up his stomach muscles and round his back. This allows him to travel with his neck surfed out, long and relaxed.

A rider who perches in the saddle, braces against the stirrups, and doesn't give the horse the kind of leg support it needs creates a horse that will likely travel with a "hollow back," which means it is arched downward. The head, neck, and shoulders will be rigid.

Although there certainly is work to be done from the bridle, the days of bitting a horse's face straight back to his chest with some sort of headsetting gimmick and working him hour after hour in a round pen are gone. The secret to attaining a proper headset is instead through the use of lateral work. I ask for only moments of proper headset, gradually increasing the time that the horse actually maintains his head and neck in a show pen position. The lateral work your horse began learning in the first few rides, such as giving his head to the direction of the circles and serpentines, has set him up with the foundation to achieving the coveted level topline. And here's a secret you might not have realized. You have been working on the headset all along with the lateral work you have been doing. All that previous work set the stage for achievement of the head and neck carriage necessary for the show pen. Now, you just need to polish it.

By the time I start this work, I have a good idea of how much yield to the bit the horse has. All of my foundation work up to this point has concentrated on the horse responding to bit pressure. Some horses take longer to get to the point where they can consistently maintain a level topline, keep their shoulders up, and maintain balance. A horse with a long, thin neck seems to be the type that comes along a little more slowly in this work. The neck is so very long that it creates a balance point out in front of the shoulders and body. With such a horse, *short-term* use of a martingale might help. The martingale helps direct the neck down when bit pressure is applied. The work must still be done laterally, rather than by pulling straight back.

I use an unsecured martingale in this case. Unsecured means that it doesn't touch anywhere on the neck; there is no breast or neck plate. It is shaped like a fork, and comes up between the horse's front legs from a snap in the middle of the girth. It's adjusted loosely enough so that it doesn't force the horse's head down, but rather stops him from raising it higher than your desired finished topline. I want the horse to learn to lower his neck when I put pressure on the reins rather than bowing his neck and moving his chin back toward his chest.

If a martingale is temporarily necessary, it should be used only for a few days, possibly up to a week. The minute the horse starts to overflex, breaking at the poll instead of the withers, and bringing his chin down toward the chest, stop using it. Overuse can instill this bad habit as well as develop a dependency on a device that cannot be used in the show arena. But, for a few rides, a martingale often helps to get the point across to a horse that is having difficulty consistently balancing with his head and neck within the level topline boundary.

Whether or not the horse is in a martingale, all I want in the beginning of this work is to keep his head and neck carriage within a fairly generous boundary. It has some give to it. Rigidly using your hands to hold the horse's neck down into one position gains nothing. Each time the neck comes up out of the boundary, I check or swing the horse's head and neck to one side, then the other. If the horse lowers his neck, I release all rein pressure as a reward. There is no "holding on." Let me stress that I am asking him to lower the neck in terms of inches, not feet.

As soon as the horse is within the generous boundary, and knows to lower his neck when bit pressure is applied, I begin to narrow the boundary and increase the amount of time I ask the horse to hold the headset, in order to establish more of a show pen carriage. I start demanding within a week that he maintain this head and neck carriage for longer intervals. I do so by asking through bit pressure for his neck to lower, then releasing the rein pressure once he does. If he elevates his head and neck, I immediately reapply rein pressure and keep him moving forward.

I don't go around and around endlessly on the rail asking for a headset. Rather, I use cross-over exercises, calisthenics work, transitions, serpentines, and circles. Repetitively maintaining the desired head carriage this way teaches the horse to find his center of balance through a relaxed neck carriage no matter what the exercise or gait. The ultimate goal of self-carriage can't be attained if the rider constantly hangs on the horse's reins in an attempt to force him to set his head.

Everything the horse has learned about using his shoulders, rounding his back, and driving with his hindquarters now helps him balance his head and neck. Every day that you ride him, he'll become better at self-carriage.

Perfecting the Show Back

During previous training I backed the horse as the last move of every ride, but I didn't worry too much about the position of the head or how straight and balanced the backup was. As long as the horse gave to the bridle and performed the maneuver calmly, I was satisfied. Now, I start to concentrate on keeping the horse's topline flat as he steps straight back. A green horse will sometimes drop his head as he starts to back up, or he will elevate his head and neck and move more from the bridle pressure rather than from the rider's leg cues. I want the backup to come totally from the use of my leg aids, which in turn causes the horse to round his back and maintain a

Check Right

As I serpentine the horse, I work laterally and use direct rein pressure to swing his head and neck first in one direction and then in the other. He gives to the bridle and brings his head back in the direction of the point of the shoulder. When he lowers his neck, I release rein pressure and keep him moving forward.

Check Left

Release and move the horse forward.

level topline. My cue for this is sitting down in the saddle and using solid leg pressure, "fixing" the reins in position without pulling, and issuing a voice command. My voice command for the backup is a kind of ticking sound made by snapping my tongue against clenched teeth.

At first, I have to use some pull-and-release rein pressure to get the horse started, then add the leg pressure and voice command. But the horse will soon get the idea from the leg and voice aids, and I can wean him off the rein cue. By backing off my legs instead of the bridle, the horse becomes responsible for his carriage without the bit intervening. His neck and topline can then stay more relaxed and therefore more level.

THE IMPORTANT Ss

◄〇►

Seasoning for Sights, Sounds, and Spookamollies and Stabling at Shows

Regardless of how much physical training is done at home, the horse will also need mental training to prepare him for the commotion at the shows. This is a whole new world for a young horse and it is up to the rider to help him deal with it.

To help season a young horse, I'll take him along to the big shows, even if he's had only a few months of riding time. He comes along for the ride early in the season and learns the routine without the added pressure of actually being shown.

A horse that has never been off the farm and is taken to a horse show environment will often come out of the trailer fresh and ready to react to everything he sees. It pays to take such a horse right to the longeing area and work him on a longe line for fifteen to thirty minutes, until he is able to calm down and begins to think straight. I don't overreact, and I don't dish out strong discipline. I merely help him get the edge off. I then take him to his stall, where I leave him tied until he completely calms down and settles in. He has been tied to the wall so much at home that he knows it is a time to conserve energy and relax.

I make a point to stable my young horse in a stall next to a quiet, older horse, making sure that all the barn buddies have a view of one another. This arrangement promotes confidence in the young horse by maintaining herd dynamics.

Even though horse shows are hectic, there are always times during the day and in the evening when things quiet down and I can take a young horse out into a warm-up pen. Depending on how far along he is in his training, I will longe, pony, or ride him. I keep things positive and safe.

If I can find a time when the actual show arena is open for practice and is not crowded, I will longe a young horse there to get him used to such "spookamollies" as the announcer's stand. When I put him on the longe line, if he wants to cut in ten feet toward me when he passes that stand, I just move ten feet closer to encourage him to move back toward it. He knows from his personal space lessons that he's not to crowd me. Because I don't react or make a huge deal out of the fact that he's spooking at the announcer's stand, he'll see that I am confident and there's nothing harmful about it. Soon he'll go right by without fretting. If I were to overreact through body language that said, "Yikes! Look at that!" the horse would think, "Oh! My owner's afraid of that horrible thing! It's going to eat me!"

When the time comes that I can ride the horse into the arena, my philosophy of not overreacting still holds true. If he spooks, I put him into a cross-over exercise or another calisthenic he knows well. His attention is redirected to what I'm asking him to do, and he forgets he was ever nervous about the "spooky place."

The minute one overreacts, the horse instinctively kicks into his fight-or-flight response. That's why staying calm and diverting his attention is wise. When a young horse is first taken to a show environment, this theory will be put into practice frequently.

Around the show grounds and on the rail of the warm-up pen there are likely to be small children playing with toys; folks throwing empty soft drink containers into metal trash cans; teenagers waving and shouting at approaching friends. A noisy tractor will pass through a gate to drag the arena, followed by a water truck with a thick spray billowing out the sides. The list of spooky distractions is endless. When a young horse spooks and elicits a panic reaction from his rider, the situation becomes far more of a problem than if the rider had simply ignored it.

Ponying a young horse is one way to condition him to all the sights and sounds. Using a well-broke, quiet horse, lead the youngster around the warm-up pen and through the show grounds. If he wiggles around at the end of the lead rope, ignore the problem and don't discipline any more than necessary to remain in control.

Be aware that when ponying, you now have two horses to maneuver through traffic. It takes a lot of rider coordination to do this. If you don't feel capable of handling the situation in a safe manner, ask someone who is experienced to pony your young horse at the show. Then, you can practice at home until you get the technique mastered.

Choosing the First Show to Exhibit in the Hunter Under Saddle Class

After hauling to a few horse shows to familiarize the young horse with the commotion of the horse show environment, begin preparing for a show you will actually exhibit in. When the sights and sounds of the horse show environment no longer overly excite the young horse, he will be ready to show in a class. Many breed shows have what is known as a "schooling warm-up" class before the Hunter Under Saddle classes begin. This is an ideal situation for the young and inexperienced horse. This class allows the riders to work at will in the company of other riders all going in the same direction. Regardless of the gait the announcer has called, you can work at whichever gait you wish; you can even stop and back your horse if he speeds up in traffic. It is important to pay attention in this class so that your schooling does not interfere with anyone else's schooling or their ride.

If the schooling class goes well, then continue the training progression and show in the Hunter Under Saddle class that is appropriate for you and your horse. Some shows have Green Hunter Under Saddle classes for the first-year horse that has never been shown, Junior Hunter Under Saddle class for horses five years and younger, or Senior Hunter Under Saddle for horses six years and older. The riders in these classes are more than likely professional trainers. However, if you are more comfortable showing with peers of a similar riding level, there are Novice, Youth, and Amateur Hunter Under Saddle classes to select from.

Some strategy can go into picking the first show to start a young horse's show career. Choosing a show that is held at a quiet show facility—one that does not have the show arena next to a busy street, racecar speedway, or airport—can be the best choice for a young horse. Returning to a show facility that you had previously hauled to during an earlier show or schooling show can also have great advantages. This allows the young horse some familiarization with the show facility and will help him to relax and settle into his first show performance more readily.

By spending this time seasoning your horse without the pressure of competition, the transition between hauling the horse to shows for experience to eventually competing in a show will go more smoothly. The key is try to prepare for the situations you have control over, for example which show facility to go to, so that any situation beyond your control—such as spooky bursts of static on the announcer's microphone—can be dealt with more easily.

{ 11 }

WARM-UP FOR THE SHOW PEN

◄◦►

Take advantage of options available to warm up your horse before his class at a show. There is usually a designated warm-up arena at most show grounds. Or early in the morning, quite often the very arena you'll be showing in will be available before classes are scheduled to start. A third option is more of a last-minute situation that allows extra time and the chance to expose your horse to the show pen environment. This happens when the class before yours is finished and lined up, but hasn't yet left the arena. Your class may be called into the arena early to expedite the show.

Remember, warm-up time isn't based on physical exercise alone. It also provides mental preparation for both horse and rider, giving each a chance to focus on the task ahead.

The type of horse you will show determines how much time you should spend warming up, and under what circumstances.

Warm-Up Time for a Nervous Horse

A nervous horse often becomes even more excited if ridden in traffic in a warm-up arena. By traffic, I mean that other horses in the arena will be working in all directions around you. It's not a con-

Learn to become aware of your surroundings in the warm-up arena.

trolled environment, unlike the show pen. In the warm-up arena, horses might be traveling in both directions. Some will be cutting across the middle. There might be reiners being put through run-downs and sliding stops. A practice jump for hunters and jumpers might be in use.

This hectic activity might bother a nervous horse, especially if he is quite fresh. One of the best things to do is work him on a longe line first before trying to ride him in a warm-up arena.

Do a lot of longeing and let him buck, play, and have a good time. When he settles down into a quiet trot or canter, his energy load will be decreased and he will be more receptive to subsequent warm-up time under saddle.

After he's been longed, climb aboard and spend quiet time in the saddle. Walk him around the warm-up arena, through the traffic. Keep your eyes up and always stay aware of your surroundings to keep your horse out of a bad situation. Don't trot or canter at

Two of my students spending quiet time in the warm-up arena.

first. Just walk. Don't get him excited or work him too hard. Walk him around enough so that his muscles and mind loosen up, then start him on some of the calisthenics he learned at home. For example, take him to the middle of the arena and do some cross-overs. Trot a few serpentines, then let him stand and relax. Then do more calisthenics. By mixing things up, his attention stays focused on you and not the other horses.

This instills confidence through familiarity. He has often been asked at home to do the same calisthenics. He'll think, "I know how to do that. It's easy." He won't get rattled because he knows what to do.

The Young Green Horse

Warming up a young horse is similar to working with the nervous horse except that the duration will be shorter. These youngsters can't handle a lot of ride time because they tend to lose their focus and grow physically tired.

Longe him just enough to get the edge off, then climb aboard. Concentrate on keeping the horse going forward and staying quiet. Sitting on the young horse for long periods of time causes his back to become tired and sore. Therefore, keep the ride time productive and make good use of your time in the saddle.

The Older Lazy Horse

Sometimes, it's better not to put a lot of warm-up time into an older lazy horse. This warm-up should be viewed from a standpoint of warming up muscles and arthritic management, rather than a means of getting excess energy out of the horse's system. Longeing the horse in the morning, then putting him back in the stall until shortly before the class will often be all he needs. Then, climb on and move him around just enough to get the kinks out so he doesn't trot into the arena "cold." Older horses all need to be loosened up at least a little bit right before you go into the show pen. Going from a resting state into a brisk trot won't achieve the pretty movement desired in the show pen.

Using Show Pen Time for Additional Warm-Up

Often at breed shows, you'll be asked to ride into the show pen while the previous class is lined up and being placed. This offers some free time to ride at will. Yes, there are times when you're asked to trot right in, and judging starts as you come through the gate. But if that's not the case—if the judges are busy scoring the previous class and there is some delay time—use this time wisely.

Start by trotting your horse into the pen. Your eyes should be up, and your shoulders back. You should exhibit a sense of confidence in your horse as you make your first pass by the judges, even if you're not quite sure you're actually being judged at this point. If you see that the judges are not ready to judge your class or the announcer calls for "ride at will," you can bring your horse down to a walk and settle him. Especially with the young horse that might be nervous, take this time before being judged to work on both the horse's nerves and your own. If you are nervous, the horse will pick up on your attitude. Try taking deep and relaxing breaths as you walk your horse. Slow everything down. Take this time to settle and become focused.

The opposite is true if you misjudged your warm-up time, and things went faster than you expected. The class ahead of yours was canceled, and all of the sudden you find yourself in the show pen! Your horse is not as calm as you had hoped. He's not nervous or green, he is just fresh. What's more, a big thundercloud passed overhead and there's electricity everywhere. Now your horse is feeling a little *too* fresh.

But you're in luck because show officials will still allow riders of your incoming class some preparation time on the rail. Spend that delay time trotting and cantering. Then pull the horse back down

Jan Ames rides the AQHA stallion Rise Above out of the warm-up pen. Her class will soon be called into the show pen.

After initially trotting in, Jan (in the back, along the rail) has brought Rise Above down to a walk. The previous class is being judged, and Jan is using this time to relax and settle in.

into a sitting trot to relax and bring him back to your hands and legs. When he responds and you know he's ready to focus, you should be confident about doing well in the class.

If during this last-minute preclass warm-up time your horse starts to play and becomes fractious, stop and back him up. This correction returns to the fundamentals he learned at home. However, avoid overdisciplining or overreacting in a preclass ride-at-will situation. "Big brother *is* watching," which means that even if the class hasn't started, the judge will see that you are schooling your horse. One of three scenarios might go through the judge's mind. (1) It is warm-up time, so you have the right to use it accordingly. (2) You are in the show pen and need to be showing, not schooling, even if the class hasn't yet officially started. (3) Your discipline is excessive for the show arena, and you will be excused.

These are all possible scenarios, and you never know which one will come to pass. The bottom line is that it's important to stay cool and calm if your horse plays about. Remember that you are there to show what you have on that particular day, and not what you expect to have when the horse is much more well-schooled and has reached his ultimate potential. Use the experience to take positive mental notes so that next time you can better prepare. Maybe plan on more longeing time or more time under saddle in the warm-up arena. Either way, learn from these experiences and use this knowledge to improve.

{ 1 2 }

FINISHING TOUCHES

—◄◦►—

N ot only will careful attention to detail create a "Wow" first impression when riding into the show pen, but there is also a psychological aspect connected to that presentation. A professional look will communicate a nonverbal message to the judge: "This is a horse you'll want to watch—not just in this class, but also in every other class he's exhibited in."

Let's look at the steps needed to wow the judge.

Clipping

Clip your horse at home before leaving for the show. If it's a multi-day show, a touch-up might be necessary. But for starters, get out the electric clippers and some disposable razors. Clip the hunter under saddle horse essentially the same way that a halter or western pleasure horse would be clipped. Remove excess hair on the legs with a #10 or #15 Oster blade, being careful not to produce clipper marks that can come from using dull blades, or allow the clippers to become too hot.

Switch to a #40 clipper blade for a closer cut on the areas under the jaw and around the muzzle. The same close cut is needed for the ears.

After using the electric clippers on the muzzle, put baby oil on the muzzle and go over that area with a disposable razor to remove all traces of remaining whiskers. Disposable razors also work well at removing long guard hairs around the eyes. Use one hand to cover the horse's eye to prevent touching it with the razor. Then, it's back to the electric clippers for the bridle path, the four- to six-inch clipped area between the forelock and the mane.

When the bridle path is properly clipped, it showcases the horse's head and throat latch. I pay close attention to customized clipping of this area. I use a #40 Oster blade to clip extremely close. A general rule of thumb is to clip the bridle path so that it is the same length as the horse's ear. Measure by folding the ear back onto the neck along the bridle path area. Where the ear ends, so should the bridle path.

However, there are variations to this rule. If I have a horse that is not as trim through the throat latch as I'd like, or is shorter-necked than what I'd consider ideal, I clip his bridle path back an inch or two longer. This longer bridle path gives the impression of shrinking the throat latch down to a smaller size and thus makes the neck appear longer.

I keep a shorter bridle path on a horse that has a very long neck and big ears. This downplays the length of the ears, but showcases the long neck and nice throat latch.

To Braid or Not To Braid

A lot of thought should go into whether or not to braid. The level of competition is often the determining factor. If attending a major show, your horse should be braided. If going to a smaller show, the decision should be based on which classes are entered and the "silent communication" you want to have with the judge.

Here is a typical scenario. You are competing at a small weekend show with your Western-type horse. He is well-broke and seasoned and you want to try for the all-around award, so you will also need to earn some points in the Hunter Under Saddle division.

You might choose Western classes such as Showmanship, Western Pleasure, Horsemanship, Western Riding, and Trail, all of which may be before the Hunter Under Saddle classes. His mane should be *banded* (no braids, just sections of small ponytails—the style used

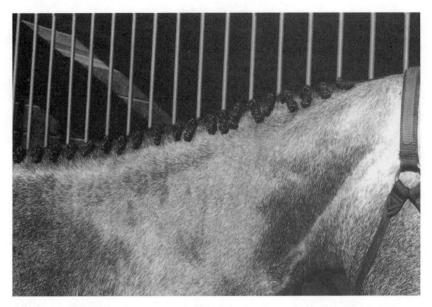

Give enough thought about your decision whether or not to braid a mane.

for Western classes) rather than braided, for those Western-oriented classes. There is nothing wrong with leaving those bands in and not braiding him for the Hunter Under Saddle classes. By riding that banded stock-type horse in the Hunter Under Saddle class, you silently convey a message to the judge. "This is my Western horse. You saw us in the Western classes this morning, and now you're going to see us in Hunter Under Saddle, because this horse can also perform well when ridden hunt seat."

Looking at the opposite scenario, let's say you have a well-broke, specialized English horse that is tall and leggy and obviously a hunter type. But they are giving a big prize at this show for the all-around award and you want to try to win it, so you also need to show your horse in some Western classes. A good class combination for a horse like this is Showmanship, Western Horsemanship, Western Riding, Trail, Hunt-Seat Equitation, and Hunter Under Saddle. In this case, braid his mane, which says to the judge, "This is my hunter. He's a big, wonderful mover. Watch him do well in these

Western classes, then look for him in the Hunter Under Saddle class because he'll be there."

When to Braid

How far in advance of the show you braid the horse's mane depends on how well you can braid. After a lot of practice and work at perfecting my braiding skills, I can braid the day before the show and usually leave them in for up to four days before redoing them. Not only do my braids stay in, because they are properly done, but also because I keep Sleazy hoods on the horses when they're not being worked or shown. The snug-fitting hood keeps the braids in place and also keeps shavings from collecting in them.

At big shows, however, I'll often rebraid each evening before a performance so the horse has a superclean look for the next day's classes.

Following tradition, I like the braids to fall on the right side of the neck. I braid with nylon yarn. Cotton yarn will break when tightening the knots. Braiding with yarn also gives a cleaner, more professional look. I think it's acceptable to braid with rubber bands, but a nicer look is achieved if an expert braider teaches you how to braid with yarn.

If you can't do it yourself, hire someone at the show. There's almost always a professional braider with a sign posted. If not, ask around at other barns about who braids their horses. What you spend on a nice braid job, which can take up to an hour and a half, is definitely worth the expense and time.

Tails

Unless I am showing at a major event such as a big futurity or a world show, I don't usually consider braiding the tail, as long as the horse has upper tail hairs that will lie flat and straight. Even at smaller shows, however, if the horse has unruly, fuzzy upper tail hair, braiding might be the only thing that can be done to keep that part of the tail neatly in place.

Normally, though, tail braiding is not something that one must do. While you will sometimes see braided tails on horses showing over fences, you won't see much of it on the flat in the Hunter Under Saddle classes.

There is no rule that says one must use an artificial tail, also called a tail extension, but there are many advantages. An artificial tail adds weight and by doing so helps drop a tail so the horse carries it in a flatter position at the top. This carriage looks much nicer than a horse that holds his tail up and away from his buttock.

If your horse has a nice low and flat tail carriage by nature, but has a thin tail, a switch-type tail extension adds bulk and volume by mixing the natural and artificial hair and creates a nicer, fuller look for the hindquarters.

There are many types of artificial tails that tie in differently, from the switch that attaches below the tailbone, to the type that has a strip of hide that lays right on top of the horse's tailbone. It is braided in with a "hair-to-hair" technique, mixing the natural and artificial hair into small braids to join them securely. Properly attached, these look extremely nice and full. When the horse moves his tail, the artificial tails moves with it and it all looks natural.

Artificial tails are a sound investment. When taken care of, they last a long time. The important thing, however, is to get a good match on color so it doesn't look like a bad wig. It needs to be tied in correctly, an art that can be learned from the person who sells the artificial tails. Vendors are oftentimes at horse shows. Or, if doing an Internet search under "tail extensions," you will find sites that have full instructions with photos.

Be sure to check your governing rulebook. Rules will vary with different breed associations, and you'll need to know the guidelines that govern the show you will be attending. Some breed associations, for example the Appaloosa Horse Club, allow only switches that are attached below the bone.

Last-Minute Enhancements

Before going into the show pen, use the same finish techniques and products as used in the showmanship class. There are products avail-

Blanche stands quietly as I attach her tail extension.

able, both in liquid and chalk forms, that can be used to enhance different equine hair colors. Check equine supply catalogs or online tack shops to see the types available. For example, on a horse with black legs, use a hair highlighter that will accentuate black. This is especially striking on gray horses with black legs, or a bay that may have two short socks with black hair above them.

Hoof black also adds contrast and finish. This is important because judges want to see the horse's legs in action, so defining and enhancing them is a good idea, especially if the horse is a nice mover. However, when riding an Appaloosa under the governing body of the Appaloosa Horse Club, clear hoof polish, not black, is to be used.

Highlighting the face is another attention getter, especially on a pretty-headed horse. Options include equine face makeup, oil, or chalk. I tend to use chalk with my hunt-seat horses, especially the ones with a great deal of Thoroughbred breeding. These animals are quite sensitive, and if their muzzles are highlighted with oil, they'll try to rub it off on their legs, possibly during the class. Imag-

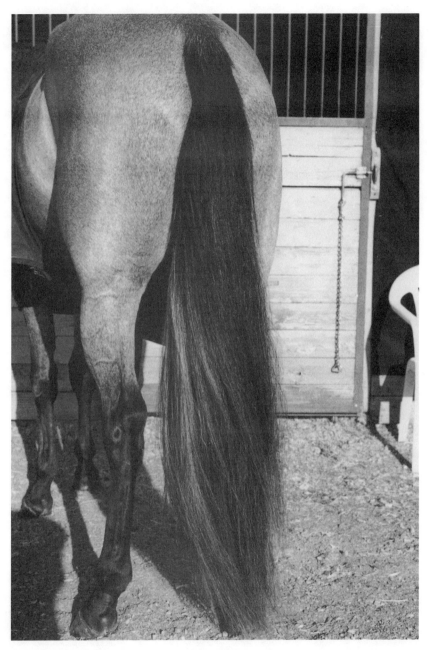

The finished product is a full, natural-looking tail.

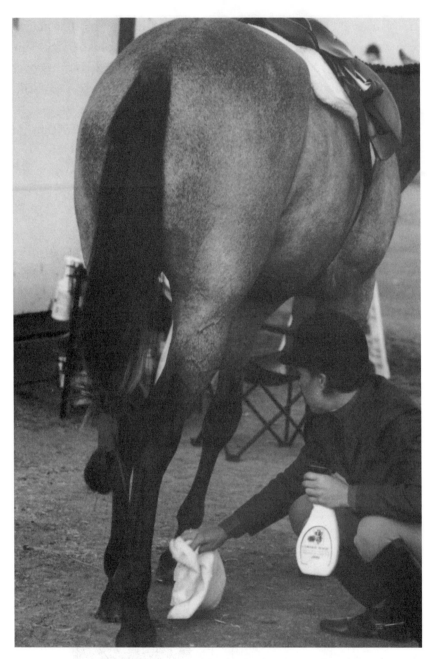

Black legs can be highlighted to produce a finished look. They should also be wiped clean before the class.

ine your own face on a warm day, coated with baby oil that begins to run. You, too, would want to wipe it off. On an older or less sensitive horse that doesn't mind the oil, the glossy shine is attractive. But if you think face makeup or oil will bother your horse, use chalk. It's dry and doesn't sweat off.

Another problem with oil occurs when showing in an outside arena. Not only will oil draw dirt to the horse's nose, a white nose on a bright, hot day will be susceptible to severe sunburn. Sunscreen might be a better product of choice.

Call the Bucket Brigade

After the horse is ready to show and you are on his back, headed to the waiting area near the show pen, it's helpful if someone is on foot to bring along a bucket full of brushes and rags, and that ever-important fly spray. A lot of dust and many flies can find you on your way to the show pen. While waiting at the arena gate for your class to be called, helpers can wipe out the horse's nostrils, so that

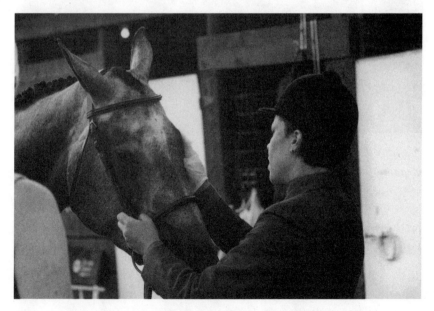

Such details as wiping dust from around the eyes are also important.

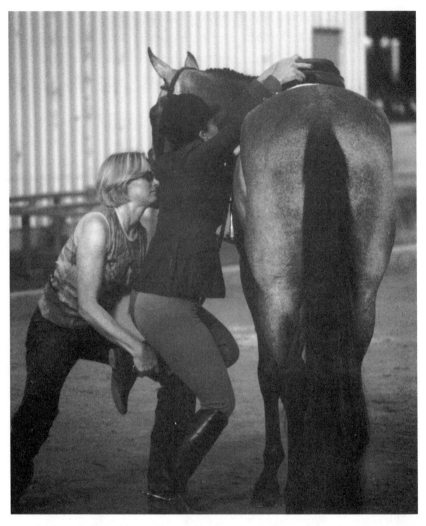

It's "ally-oop" into the saddle, and away we go to the show pen. The "bucket brigade" will follow us to the in-gate waiting area.

he isn't thinking about a drippy nose during the class. They can also run a soft rag over the horse right before showtime, to remove any dust that might have sailed over from a warm-up pen. They can smooth out a tail, or fix a wayward braid. Helpers are invaluable. Let them know they're appreciated.

DRESSING FOR SHOW PEN SUCCESS

———◄◦►———

It's certainly not a fashion show, but dressing correctly for a Hunter Under Saddle class adds to the overall professional picture. Though there is some room for adding color, compared to what is seen in Western classes, the look is more restrained.

Before putting together an outfit, read the rulebook for the breed association that will govern the shows you plan to attend. There will be specific guidelines to follow. For example, at the time this was written, AQHA's rulebook asked for hunt coats of such traditional colors as navy, dark green, gray, black, or brown. Maroon and red were considered improper. Breeches or jodhpurs were to be traditional shades of buff, khaki, canary, light gray, or rust. These rules also specified that hunt boots or paddock boots should be black or brown, and hunt caps should be black, brown, or navy blue.

Because of the conservative nature of the English style, don't expect these rules to change much.

Boots and Caps

Over the years, I've found that black boots and hunt caps have remained the most popular and acceptable for use in the hunter under saddle pen. They look nice with every color of horse, and add

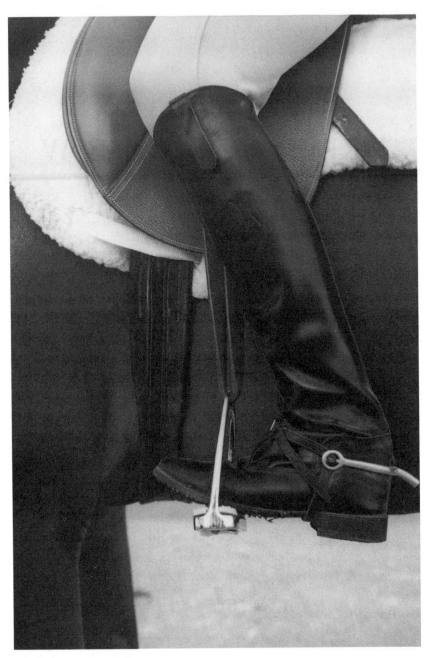

Black boots look nice against a horse of any color.

a formal look to the overall picture. Either field or dress hunt boots are acceptable. ASTM-approved (American Society for Testing and Materials) hunt caps with harnesses are optional when showing on the flat, but mandatory when schooling or showing over fences.

Breeches

Consider the color of your horse when choosing breeches. For example, rust breeches paired with a blue-gray horse don't look nice, but dress in gray breeches and the picture becomes more striking. On the Open USA Equestrian (formerly AHSA) circuit, the most accepted color of breeches is khaki, no matter what color the horse. Khaki is considered the standard.

Fads race through the industry like wildfire, and everyone seems to rush out and buy the same color breeches. But don't let that keep you from buying breeches that will look good against the color of your horse.

Hunt Coats

Horse color should also be a factor in deciding what color coat to wear. I ride many horses, so I have several coats to choose from. I like the look of a blue-gray coat with a gray, bay, or black horse, but I don't think it looks good with a palomino or sorrel. These horses look best with hunter green, navy blue, or dark brown.

Hunt coats must be fitted well through the shoulders and waist, especially for women who have defined waistlines and want to accentuate that feature. It's distracting to see a hunt coat that is obviously too large or small. If you have a full figure, you should still have a smooth coat fit. Try to avoid the sloppy look that comes with a coat that is too large or the "tug and pull" appearance of a coat that is too small.

Gloves

Gloves the same color as the hunt cap and boots can be worn. Black gloves are the most popular and add a formal finishing touch to

The color of your horse should be a factor in your choice of your hunt coat color.

hunt-seat attire. Gloves also downplay the movement of a rider's hands.

Shirt and Choker Basics

The guidelines I follow for showing at AQHA events will give you some ideas about shirts and chokers. Be sure to check your governing rulebook for the type of shirt and choker it calls for.

In the hunter under saddle classes, louder shirt colors can help distinguish competitors from one another on the rail. This is the one place where subtle tradition has stepped aside. Of course, attire still needs to be conservative in equitation classes, but for the hunter under saddle class you're trying for some distinction. A maroon shirt in a subdued tone, a soft or dark blue, or perhaps a pale yellow shirt can be worn. Green with a medium white pinstripe is nice as well. These "louder" colors, along with heavier pinstripes, will help give attention to the total picture being presented.

For ladies, the choker that comes with your shirt is the best bet for neckwear. It should be the same material as the shirt. Some people prefer adding a monogram or an area with small detail on the choker. Pins used to be all the rage, but seem to have fallen off in popularity over the years, though they are still appropriate.

Men often wear white shirts but dress up the outfit with color in the form of a conservative tie.

Jewelry, Hair, and Caps

Earrings must be small and understated for the hunter under saddle arena. Ladies must have their hair up under the cap, or tied back in a tight bun. Hair should not hang below the collar or swing wildly in a ponytail. In addition to being sloppy, it makes the horse look as though he's moving rough.

Even if your hair is nicely contained and your hunt cap fits snugly on your head, big, gaudy, swinging earrings are a definite distraction to the overall picture. And you don't want to ride into the show pen with fourteen ear piercings and a nose ring! Remember, the hunt-seat attire must remain conservative.

Easy on the Makeup

There have been television sitcom characters over the years who have piled on makeup to the point that they have a cartoonlike appearance. Being attractively made up is one thing, but looking like a clown has no place in the show pen. Pleasant makeup is part of the overall picture. You don't want your appearance to be overdone or offensive.

Undergarments

Some of today's breeches are made from material that is lightweight and more comfortable than the heavy breeches of days gone by. That's the good news. The bad side is that attention is drawn to any cellulite and visible panty lines. I suggest that riders wear panty hose under breeches to smooth things out.

For those women with an ample bust, wearing a high-quality sports bra will keep everything still. And if you're a larger woman who needs a corset to smooth out the midsection, don't hesitate to purchase one.

The bottom line is that you are showing in the hunter under saddle class to showcase your horse. Keep your attire, makeup, hair, and jewelry conservative and quiet so your judge is not distracted. He needs to see the entire picture as a balanced and beautiful image.

{ 14 }

RIDING THE HUNTER UNDER SADDLE CLASS

━━━◄◦►━━━

Two possible scenarios can come into play when it's time to begin riding the class. The first is mentioned in the chapter on warming up. That is when the previous class is still in the middle of the pen being scored, and your class is allowed into the arena to ride at will. The other scenario is when judging begins as the horses enter through the gate at the trot.

In the first scenario, I pay close attention to how much time I have before the start of my class, based on how many horses from the previous class are still in the pen. As those horses are placed and begin to leave the arena, I can get an idea of how long it will be before they have all left and my class officially starts. I also calculate how much horse I have regarding freshness, energy load, age, and strength.

I will begin trotting a young, green horse well before the announcer calls for my class to take the rail at the trot. It takes a younger horse longer to establish pace and cadence. The trade-off is that it's important to know the horse's capabilities so that I don't wind up "running out of horse" halfway through the class.

If I'm riding a well-seasoned horse that is mentally and physically ready to go, I might wait for the class to begin before starting to trot, particularly if he's a lazy horse that tires easily. If he has enough stamina, I pick up the trot before the class officially begins so I can show-

If your class is in the arena before the previous class is dismissed, watching how quickly those horses leave will give you an idea of how soon your own class will start.

case his movement to the judge, once he has turned his attention away from the previous class. These are two of the last-minute judgment calls I must be prepared to make. I can't make them until I am actually on the horse and can feel what needs to be done. You too will have to learn to "read your horse" to make the right decisions.

In the second scenario, the show pen is clear and my class was not called in when the previous class was being placed. I must then begin the class from outside the arena.

First and foremost, I assess the safety of the show pen's entry gate. Does it have a metal support pole on the ground that a horse could trip over? Does it have a metal support overhead that I'll need to duck under? These are problems that are faced with the uncoordinated young horse or the very tall horse. I have shown in arenas with overheads so low that in order to enter the arena I had to lie on the horse's neck to clear the gate. Once in the arena, I was then able to sit upright and start the trot.

If a gate is easily passable, the next issue is how experienced the horse is. An older horse will be able to enter the arena from a short distance and establish cadence quickly. But a younger, green horse might be intimidated by the gate and will suck back or balk when he sees the vacant arena. This young horse should not go in first, but should be paced behind a more steady competitor as they enter through the gate. Following the other horse into the arena will instill confidence in the youngster.

Another consideration in entering the show pen is how much space is available outside the gate in which to acquire the trot. Some arenas are designed with very little dirt space and are often bordered by concrete. Since it is dangerous to trot a horse on any concrete surface, I prefer to start my horse on the small dirt space and pick up a slower trot just to get through the gate, then accelerate to the desired trot once inside the arena.

Riding in the Small Class

Especially if you're showing in a Junior or First Year Green class at a weekend show, there is a possibility that only three or four horses will be judged. In this scenario of a big arena with a small number of entries, it is common to see all of them end up bunched together, herding up as they circle the pen.

As both an exhibitor and a judge, I prefer to see a small class well spaced out and not packed together. Even as a spectator, it frustrates me to see everybody in the same small space. One horse passes, and another horse passes—so much competition for herd behavior takes away from the performance of each horse. A judge who starts to see this scene loses the vantage point of being able to view each horse's movement individually.

There's also a problem when the announcer calls for riders to "use half the arena." Nobody seems to know just where the dividing line is. It might be half the arena when the first horse makes the turn, but when the second horse comes around the "half" is shortened by another ten feet. The same thing happens with the third

Even in a small class, it is important to find the best spacing possible so the judge can get a clear view of your horse. Jan Ames is doing an excellent job staying visible to the judge as she rides Rise Above in an amateur class.

horse, and by the time the fourth horse comes around he's making a little circle around the judge.

An exhibitor in this situation loses the horse's length of stride, the horse's focus, and cadence. Horses don't show well when the arena is cheated.

In a small class, strive for the best spacing you can get. Your horse will perform better. The judge will be able to see how your horse moves and evaluate that movement without being distracted by others fighting for the same place on the rail.

Riding in Large Classes

When watching a hunter under saddle class, you've probably noticed that riders often keep their horses off the rail more than in the Western pleasure classes. There's a good reason.

Most arenas are either square or rectangular. A Western pleasure horse is not striving for a long, low forward stride, so riding deep into each corner can be useful as a slow-down and collection tool if necessary.

But with a hunter under saddle horse, consistent length and extension of stride all the way around the arena is optimal. Riding the arena in an imaginary long oval shape will help maintain an even cadence and length of stride. To ride too deep into the corners causes a loss in stride length. His cadence becomes insufficient, and he appears to move in a choppy, erratic style as he slows down in the corner and then speeds up as he returns to the long wall. The ideal? Make a nice arc around the short wall so that you maintain the length of stride and keep the horse's shoulders up.

Riding the arena as an oval instead of a rectangle helps you keep your horse in even cadence and length of stride. I'm turning Blanche long before I reach the corner of the arena so that I can keep her traveling in that oval.

We also ride away from the rail in part so we're not always pulling out to pass someone, which will also interrupt the horse's stride. I like to ride ten to fifteen feet off the rail on a path in a long oval, in a quest to promote an even cadence. Coming off the wall any further is not productive because the area covered becomes too small. A rider who is too far off the wall rotates around the center of the arena; the judge can't see the horse well, because it's too close for him to evaluate the topline and way of going. The judge looks up and there, twenty feet in front of him, is a big 16-hand-plus horse. The scope of the judge's vision is so narrow at that distance that he doesn't get to see the prettiness of the horse's floating trot, or the nice cadenced canter. That is why some judges are starting to penalize riders who ride too far off the rail.

Another consideration is sportsmanship. Take into consideration how your position on or off the rail affects your fellow exhibitors. If you're cutting your corners too much, you drive others into the center when they are trying to pass.

I prefer riding off the rail, instead of right on it.

Ride a Gap

I tell my students to "ride a gap," especially in a big class. This means keeping ample distance from the horses ahead and behind you. To keep that gap takes quick thinking. For example if you are closing in on the horse ahead of you and do not want, or do not have, the room to pass, ride a little closer to the rail and allow that horse and rider to cut the corners and stay ahead of you. If, however, you notice that a crowd of horses is about to overtake you, you can ride a little further from the rail and cut the corners to stay ahead of the pack, and therefore remain in clear view of the judge. It's easy to see who is ahead of you, but it takes more effort to watch who is coming up from behind. One of the best ways to check on approaching horses is to take advantage of the end of your imaginary oval when you are making the turn around the short wall of the arena. You can move your head around slightly and spot the other horses with your

I tell my students to "ride a gap" and keep ample distance between the horse in front of them and the horse behind.

peripheral vision. You're still looking into your turn, but in a sense you get a "rearview mirror" glance. To turn all the way around to look behind while traveling down the long side of the arena takes the focus off the communication you're trying to keep with the horse. This movement could also throw the horse off balance.

The more you can stay equally spaced, the better your horse will go. If the herd is behind you, your young horse might become rattled as other horses pass him. Once they all bunch up and get that herd behavior going, they are prone to lose communication with their riders, lose their focus, and do what's instinctive to them—stay packed close to the other herd members.

For the best class spacing, everyone needs to make an effort to ride in his or her own gap. While it is all right to pass or to be passed, a rider should not be consumed with passing the next horse ahead as if in a race. Hunter under saddle classes aren't judged on which horses trot the fastest, but rather on which ones move the best. Therefore, show your horse at his best pace and cadence, and allow the other exhibitors to do the same. By doing so, troublesome traffic jams can easily be managed or avoided.

Using Transition Timing to Keep Your Gap

Another method of assuring good spacing is to take advantage of the preparation time given for a transition departure. For example, the announcer calls for the canter from a walk. The horse in front is very close, but there is a lot of space behind. Stay at the current gait (in this case, the walk) to give the horse in front a head start. When he's far enough ahead to give a gap, ask your horse for the canter.

The same holds true if your horse is in front, and another competitor is tailgating. You should pick up the canter first, which will give some distance and establish space for the horse that is behind. Consideration of other riders should always be on your mind, as well as being aware of the judge's time and patience. Don't drag the transition out so long that the judge must wait an excessive amount of time to see your transition. Transitions should be completed at, or very shortly after, the announcer's call.

Ride to Help the Inexperienced Horse

There is an instance when I alter the old "here's-where-your-hands-stay-in-hunt-seat" rules. It takes many classes before a green horse establishes consistency and becomes more proficient in self-carriage. A young horse will often need a little help, which I gladly give him. I will ride him with my hands about eighteen inches apart. A young green horse that is not yet balanced and down on the bit requires more lateral help to maintain the desired neck and shoulder position.

With a stronger, older, and more broke horse that is already proficient in self-carriage, I use the more traditional hand position. Holding my hands closer together allows me to ride with a more appropriate position since this horse won't require as much assistance.

I will ride a green horse with my hands about eighteen inches apart to help them balance down on the bit. This is Blanche cantering at her third show.

Altering the way you post can improve a horse's way of going as well. Posting rhythm will determine the timing of your horse's legs. For example, if you are posting quickly, your horse will probably trot too fast, known as "trotting off his feet." He will almost look as if he wants to break into a canter from the trot. But, when you slow your posting by sitting a little longer in the saddle on each "down" motion, the horse's legs will slow down. This reduction in posting speed allows the opportunity to build his length of stride instead of the speed of his legs.

The horse will travel with a tighter hock if the rider sits back a little more through the post rather than assuming the truly forward-seat position of a rider jumping over fences. Teaming that "sit-back" position with a change in posting rhythm will give the power to control the horse's stride through the rider's seat aids.

Individualize the posting cadence to the horse's requirements. Don't look to other riders for examples. Base your posting on the feel and the needs of your own horse. For example, a rider on a tall, hunter-type horse is going to post slower than someone riding a 15-hand Western-type horse that lacks the long, extended, floaty trot stride.

When the Judge Calls for a Backup

Sometimes at the end of the class horses are lined up in the center of the pen and asked to back. This is usually the case if the judge or judges are going to check bits, which they do to be sure all are "legal" within the breed association's rules. However, at many breed shows, riders are asked to stop their horses on the rail and back up. This is where your daily home schooling on the show back can be most beneficial.

Although I can't say that the backup holds a lot of weight in most judges' final scores, I think a horse that really resists and does not back well can and should be penalized and placed below a horse, with a similar rail performance, that comes back off the bri-

Often at breed shows, riders are asked to stop and back their horses on the rail.

dle without resistance. Even a horse that was the best mover in the class, if he shows that much resistance in backing up, should have points taken away from his total score.

As judges, I don't think we're doing justice to the industry when the winner of a class throws his head upside down, hollows his back, braces, and refuses to back up. This is especially true if there were other horses in the class that moved just as well and were not resistant in their backup maneuvers.

Standing Quietly

Whether riders are asked to stop and then stand on the rail during the class or to ride to the center and stand after the class is over, a horse looks best when kept in a proper frame until all judges' cards have been turned in.

I prepare my horses by standing them for three to ten minutes when I'm training at home, sometimes on the rail, other times in

When the class is over and riders are asked to line up in the center of the arena, they should keep their horses standing in a frame until the judge has turned in his card.

the middle of the arena. Regardless of where I ask for this halt, the horse must stand still and stay framed. Whether competing or as a judge, I like to see a horse stand quietly, with his neck level and his mouth relaxed, rather than lifting his head like a giraffe to gawk all around.

The ability to hold the horse in a frame, whether on the rail or in the middle of the arena, adds a touch of professionalism and showmanship to the complete show pen picture.

Know What Can Go Wrong in a Class

Being cut off by other riders in a class due to their inexperience or lack of attention is one of the problems you're likely to face, particularly in novice classes. Your horse may throw up his head in surprise. How do you recover? Bridle him back up, soften his mouth

I am holding Blanche in a frame, in the line up, after her Junior Hunter Under Saddle class at a Spokane, Washington show.

with your hands, and apply leg pressure to round his back to put him back into the desired frame. You can also hope that the judge saw the entire incident and understands what happened, or better yet saw nothing at all.

If the judge penalizes you because your horse reacted badly to being cut off, understand that sometimes that is just the way showing works. Try to better prepare your horse for these disasters by ponying him at home so that he's used to having another horse up close. Then ride the show pen with as much awareness as possible of the other competitors around you.

Before you become a victim, employ "defensive driving" techniques and speak to the rider who is about to cut you off. Ask for more space. Most of the time people are very sportsmanlike and, upon hearing your request, will move off and not cut in. Sometimes the person about to commit the crime is simply misjudging the cadence of your horse and thinks that you're going slower than you actually are.

Handling Disappointment

You read in the beginning of this book what happens to horses whose riders have a "first place, every time" attitude. These young horses don't stand a chance of having long, happy show careers.

If things didn't go well in a class, don't take out your disappointment on your horse. He doesn't need to feel the tension. He doesn't need to be reprimanded for being inexperienced in the show pen or for giving his all and just not fitting the "look" desired by one particular judge on one particular day.

Exhibiting your disappointment to the judge and spectators is uncalled for and could result in a reprimand from the governing association. As a trainer, I understand that some youth and amateur riders become upset with a poor performance or poor placing, but they need to learn to keep their chin up, and grin and bear it. These are all natural emotions and we've all felt them, but there is a time and place to vent them, and the show arena or surrounding areas are not that venue. Leave the show pen graciously with no outbursts or glares. Keep your disappointment confined to your camper or tack room. Judges will remember poor attitudes more readily than poor performances. Keep showing even after the showing is done. Recover your positive attitude, because you will undoubtedly have learned something from your ride. That experience will be invaluable toward winning your next class.

Congratulations, You've Come a Long Way!

Can you believe it? You have brought yourself and your horse along wonderfully by following sound training principles that began with laying a strong foundation and learning progressively through daily exercises and calisthenics. By having done so, you can enjoy your horse and feel confident that you are as well prepared as anyone in the hunter under saddle show arena.

Nevertheless, always remember that showing is a sport, with its ups and downs. A lot of things play into the equation at horse shows. Know that there will be days when you have the ride of your life and walk out of the show arena without an award, and other days when you barely cheated your horse through a class and became victorious. The days that you feel robbed will balance out with the days you feel gifted by the judges. The hunter under saddle classes can be both exhilarating and humbling. Be gracious with your successes and failures and choose to be a lifetime student of the sport. Because as long as you have learned something during your experience you have succeeded and triumphed—in a real sense, you are a winner.

GLOSSARY

――◄○►――

NOTE: Many of the terms are defined specifically by how they apply to the hunter under saddle horse. They might differ from general definitions because they are specific to the particular task.

AHSA American Horse Shows Association (now US Equestrian) The national federation and regulatory body of horse sports in the United States.

alfalfa A nutrient-rich legume used for hay.

All-around To compete for all-around honors at a horse show, a horse must be ridden in a variety of (sometimes three or more) categories. Each breed association has rules on how many events and which categories.

atlas The first cervical vertebra of the neck. The atlas is connected to balance because of its location in relation to the inner ear. When atlases are out of joint, horses exhibit leading problems and soreness in the loins.

AQHA (American Quarter Horse Association) The largest breed registry and association for Quarter Horses. Website: www.aqha.com

bar The space between the horse's incisors and lower molar teeth that accommodates the bit. Also, the part of the hoof between the toe and the heel.

barn sour See "sour."

barrel The midsection of a horse, between the heart girth and the flank.

beat The number of footfalls at a gait. The walk is a four-beat gait, the trot has two beats, and the canter or lope has three.

bell boot A rubber boot worn on the front pastern to protect against interference due to overreaching.

billet One of the straps on a saddle to which the girth or cinch is buckled. All-purpose and competition saddles have three billet straps, of which two are used and the third is a spare.

bolt To run away, usually out of control. Bolting often results from an unexpected sight or sound that frightens the horse to the point of panicking.

bowed tendon An injury caused by the extensive stretching and tearing of a front leg's flexor tendon sheath. It is usually caused by repeated strain to the tendon, which then loosens from the cannon bone and develops the appearance of a taut archery bow. Although a horse with a bowed tendon can return to work, the tendon will never regain its former strength.

broke Another word for "trained." A horse that is saddle-broke has been trained to accept tack and a rider.

cadence The rhythm of a horse's stride, often used to describe the regularity of steps.

calf-kneed A conformation fault, in which the carpal joints of the forelegs bend backward. It is considered a serious conformation fault, since the knee will have a tendency to hyperextend backward. Also known as back at the knee.

check ligament The accessory ligament of the deep flexor tendon, its function is to "check" the deep flexor tendon and prevent it from overstretching. The deep flexor tendon originates at the back of the forearm just above the knee, then continues down the back of the knee, the cannon bone, fetlock, and pastern, and attaches deep within the foot to the coffin bone. The check ligament begins on the bones of the back of the knee, extends down the back of the cannon bone, and is nestled between the deep flexor tendon and cannon bone. About two-thirds of the way down the cannon bone, it fuses with the tendon.

cinchy An undesirable protest to the girth being tightened, such a pinning back ears, biting, stamping, or kicking.

close-contact saddle A saddle with little or no padding in the seat and knee flaps. The phrase refers to the close contact between the horse and rider, which allows subtle communication of the rider's seat and legs.

conformation An individual horse's physical characteristics in relation to the ideal standards of his breed or type.

contact The degree of rein pressure against the horse's mouth.

coronary band The upper part of the foot by which the outer hoof wall is connected to the leg.

cribbing An undesirable habit in which a horse clamps his teeth onto a solid object (such as the edge of a feed bin) and sucks air into his lungs. Cribbing is often a result of boredom.

cross-fire In the canter, rather then staying on the same lead with both the inside front and hind legs, the horse "drops his lead" with one of those legs. For example when cantering to the left, the horse is on the left lead in front and the right lead in back. Also known as "cross-canter" or "disunited canter."

croup The top of the rump from loin to dock.

curb chain (or strap) A chain (or strap) worn with a curb bit or shank snaffle, under the horse's jaw, to increase the bit's leverage effect.

cutter (cutting horse) A Western event in which the horse separates a cow from the herd and prevents it from returning.

deep-hocked A horse that is deep-hocked and engaged in the hindquarters brings his hind legs deep underneath his belly, using his hindquarters to drive forward. He pushes himself around the arena, rather than pulling himself with his front end. That forward propulsion allows him to elevate and use his shoulders, which, in turn, produces a flat-kneed look. Each time a hind leg comes forward, the hock swings deeply under the horse's body.

direct rein   Rein pressure created by the rider's hand being drawn out to the side and/or back toward the hip of the horse, in the direction the rider wants the horse to move.

dock   The fleshy root of the tail, or "tailbone."

draw reins   A training device consisting of a pair of reins that passes from the horse's girth between the forelegs and through the bridle rings back to the rider's hands.

elbow   The joint connecting the foreleg to the body.

ElectroBraid fence   Polyester fiber fencing material in double-helix construction that works like hot wire. Because it has no sharp edges and doesn't tangle like conventional wire, it is considered very safe for horse fencing. It is also thicker and more visible than wire. Website: www.electrobraid.com

engagement   The action of the horse's hind legs that propels him with impulsion. Also known as engagement of the hocks.

extend   To increase the length of the horse's stride.

farrier   A person who shoes horses; also known as a horseshoer or blacksmith; from *fer*, the French word for "iron."

fender   The wide panel between the seat and stirrup of a Western saddle.

flat-kneed   A flat-kneed horse is loose and fluid in his motion. He does not lift his knees excessively high. Because he works off his hind end, the horse lifts his forequarters, which allows each forelimb to extend straight before landing on the ground. It is a quality prized in hunters under saddle.

float   To file down the sharp edges of a tooth to keep them from cutting into the inside of the horse's mouth.

forehand   The part of the horse in front of the barrel. *See also* heavy on the forehand.

frame   A horse's frame can best be described by using imaginary lines around his body. A correct hunter under saddle frame is when the topline of the frame is drawn from the poll (or top of

the ears) to the withers, to the croup. If the horse is moving to
the right, the right side of the frame is a line drawn at an angle
like a backslash, from the withers, through the slope of the shoulder, and down through a fully extended (forward) front leg. The
left side of the frame is a parallel backslash that extends from the
back of the buttocks, through the hock, and down through a fully
extended (forward) back leg. Therefore, the frame is a parallelo-
gram in which the horse moves.

futurity A horse show class or division for which young horses are
eligible and are nominated well in advance of the event, often up
to a year or more.

gait One of the distinctive leg movements of a horse in motion.
These include the walk, the jog or trot, the lope or canter, and
the gallop.

gapping at the mouth Opening the mouth as though trying to
spit out the bit.

girth A strap that passes under a horse's belly to secure the saddle
in place.

grass hay Any of various species of grass rich in carbohydrates, as
distinguised from protein-rich legumes.

green A "green" horse is green-broke, meaning that he is trained
to a minimum degree in comparison to a horse that is well-broke.

half halt Application of the rider's hand and leg aids to get a
momentary rebalancing from the horse. It is accomplished by a
combination of the rider applying hand and seat aids, while maintaining impulsion with the legs.

half pass A lateral movement in which the horse simultaneously
moves sideways and forward.

hand The unit by which horses are measured from the withers to
the ground. One hand equals four inches, so a horse that stands
15 hands high (abbreviated hh) measures sixty inches at the withers.

headset The position of or the way a horse carries his head. The
correct headset for a hunter under saddle is low, with his face at
the vertical.

heavy on the forehand The horse travels in an unbalanced manner because it is carrying too much of its body's weight on its forequarters, which restricts the ability to move forward with optimum impulsion.

hindquarters The portion of the horse behind the barrel.

hood A covering worn over the horse's head and neck to keep the mane lying down, and to protect the animal from dirt or insects. Is often used in the winter to provide warmth.

hoof The hard outside part of the foot. Like the human fingernail, a horse's hoof must be trimmed on a regular basis. Hooves are made of keratin, a protein substance.

Horsemanship class See Western Horsemanship class.

hunt cap The sturdy velvet-covered headgear traditionally worn by the Master of Foxhounds and hunt staff, and by competitors in hunt-seat horse show classes. Like any other protective headgear, the cap should include a well-fitting chin harness. Rulebooks of breed associations give requirements for caps in order for them to be acceptable at a show.

Hunter Under Saddle class A horse show class in which the horse is judged on its ability to move at the walk, trot, and canter in the manner of a hunter-type horse.

Hunt-Seat Equitation A horse show class in which riders are judged on form and control of their hunt-seat horsemanship. At breed shows, it includes work in a specified pattern, as well as on the rail.

impulsion Energy generated by the horse's hindquarters to produce forward thrust.

indirect rein Rein pressure created by the rider's hand on the "outside" direction of travel.

inside The side of the horse that is closer to the center of the arena, or the circle that the horse is being ridden in. If the horse is traveling left, the inside is the left side, and vice versa.

jog The Western term for a slow, collected trot.

knee The joint in the foreleg between the forearm and cannon bone.

Kimberwicke   A bit that combines the actions of both the snaffle and curb bits with a single set of reins.

lead   Determined by the foreleg and hind leg that extend furthest forward as the horse canters. When the horse is on the left lead, his left fore and hind legs will move noticeably forward of the right legs.

legume   Any of the nitrogen-rich grasses used for hay, such as alfalfa.

leg yield   Any lateral movement in which the inside fore and hind legs cross in front of the outside legs, such as the two-track or full pass.

leverage bit   A general term for a type of bit, such as a curb, that exerts pressure through the leverlike action of its sidepieces.

ligament   Fibrous tissue that connects bones as well as supporting and strengthening joints.

longe   (pronounced "lunge") To exercise a horse by having it circle around its handler at the end of a rope or line.

long yearling   A yearling that is at least eighteen months of age and will be turning two years old in the spring.

muzzle   The part of the face between the nostrils and upper lip.

neck   The part of the body that connects the head to the shoulders.

novice   Exhibitors who have not won more points than their breed show's rulebook states as the limit, before they advance to regular amateur or youth classes.

one-sided   Of a horse, working more comfortably and effectively in one direction than the other.

on the bit   A description of a horse that is accepting the bit, responsive to the rider's aids, and moving with impulsion. The horse is on the bit when the rider feels the horse reach for the bit while engaging through his body with proper impulsion and frame.

over at the knees   A conformation defect in which the upper leg arches forward from the knee when viewed from the side.

pad   A hard plastic or rubber sheet that covers and protects the sole of the foot.

pelham   A bit that has a ring and a shank on both sides and combines the effects of a curb and a snaffle.

pen   Another word for arena or riding ring.

poll   The highest portion of a horse's head, behind its ears.

ponying   Leading one horse while riding another.

posting trot   A trot to which the rider posts, or rises and sits, to the trot. It is distinguished from the sitting trot. Also called a rising trot.

pulling through the bit   Rooting the head forward, to evade bit pressure.

Quarter Horse   The most populous American breed, originally developed for ranch work. See AQHA.

reiner (reining horse)   A horse that is exhibited in the reining class, which require maneuvers such as rundowns, sliding stops, rollbacks, circles, and spins.

ring sour   See "sour"

rowel   The pointed wheel of a spur shank.

sack out   A colloquial term for training a horse not to react to a distraction. The term originated from the old-fashioned use of a burlap sack to desensitize the horse to being touched all over.

self-carriage   A horse's ability to carry himself without excessive involvement from the rider. It is much like a supermodel who has learned to carry herself in a poised, confident, beautiful manner down the runway, without constant posture reminders from a coach.

Showmanship at Halter   This class, held for youth and amateur exhibitors only, tests showmanship skills as the handler performs a pattern while leading a horse from the ground. Condition of the horse, in terms of grooming and fitting, is also judged.

Sleazy hood   Lycra stretch garment made by Sleazy Sleepwear for horses in different styles, from hoods that fit only over the head and neck, to those that extend over the shoulders. Trains and protects the horse's mane and doesn't rub the mane, because of the light weight of the material. Prevents the sun from bleaching the horse's hair when the horse is outside. Website: www.ss4horses.com

slow-legged A horse carrying himself in the correct frame utilizes his body and his stride to the fullest. Because he uses the full length of his stride and his stride is longer, his legs give the appearance of moving slowly with soft and fluid strides that push him along the ground from his hindquarters.

snubbing Restricting a horse's movement by a short, tight, strong grip on the halter rope.

sour Unhappy, usually because of boredom. A "barn sour" horse has spent too much time in the stable. A "ring sour" horse has received too much work in the arena.

stifle The joint between the thigh and gaskin. The equivalent of the human knee joint.

suspensory ligament The ligament behind the knee or the top of the hind leg cannon bone. Attached to the sesamoid bones, it supports the fetlocks.

surf A colloquial term for a horse stretching out his head and neck.

tail bag A fabric bag made to cover and protect the bottom portion of the horse's tail, from two or three inches below the base of the tailbone to the bottom of the tail.

throat latch The portion of the body between the neck and the lower jawbone.

topline The horse's upper "profile," the topline starts at the poll or the tips of his ears, continues along the top of his neck to the withers, and on to the point of his hip, or croup area. The correct topline for a hunter under saddle prospect consists of a rounded arch that goes from the poll back to the top of the hip, with the highest point being the rounded back.

Trail class This class tests the maneuverability of the horse as he works over a course of obstacles, which often include poles to walk, trot, or lope over, back through, or sidepass. Often, there is a gate that must be opened from horseback and a bridge to cross.

transition Change from one gait to another.

turn out To put a horse in a pasture, pen, or paddock where it can relax and exercise at will.

twisted wire snaffle A snaffle bit with a corkscrew-shaped mouth-piece. The wider the corkscrew's spiral, the milder the bit's effects.

Vetrap A type of self-adhering elastic bandage for medical treat-ment and to wrap legs for support.

vice Any undesirable habit, such as cribbing or weaving.

weaving Swaying from side to side, a bad habit often caused by boredom.

Western Horsemanship class This class is held for youth and amateur exhibitors and tests their horsemanship abilities. In the first section of the class, riders follow a prescribed pattern that in-cludes maneuvers at the walk, trot, or lope, and often includes a 360-degree turn and backup. Finalists in the class ride as a group on the rail, much in the same way as Western Pleasure class ex-hibitors, except that in Horsemanship the judge is scoring riders on body position, seat, and ability to control the horse.

Western Pleasure class Contestants ride this "rail class" around the arena, performing at the walk, jog, and lope in one direction, then reverse and repeat the gaits in the other direction. Horses are judged on quality and consistency of movement, calm, quiet demeanor, and the ability to travel in self-carriage on a loose rein.

Western Riding class Horses are judges on the ability to change leads easily, simultaneously, and precisely between the middle of pylons in a set pattern. The class also includes work at the walk and jog.